Rocket Ships and God

Rocco Leonard Martino, Ph.D.

Rocket Ships and God

A Scientist Puts
Faith to the Test

SOPHIA INSTITUTE PRESS
Manchester, New Hampshire

Sophia Institute Press
Box 5284, Manchester, NH 03108
1-800-888-9344

www.SophiaInstitute.com

Sophia Institute Press® is a registered trademark of Sophia Institute.

Library of Congress Cataloging-in-Publication Data
Martino, R.L.
    Rocket ships and God : a scientist puts faith to the test / Rocco Leonard
Martino, Ph.D.
        pages cm
    Includes bibliographical references.
    ISBN 978-1-62282-209-6 (pbk. : alk. paper) 1. Religion and science. I.
Title.
    BL240.3.M3985 2015
    201'.65 — dc23

2015000901

First printing

Contents

Foreword

Rocket Ships and God is a valuable book to possess. I have read it carefully, and it is obvious that the author, my good friend Dr. Rocco Leonard Martino—or Rocky, as I prefer—is a strong Catholic and proud of that fact. Rocky has been in the forefront of rocket and computer science almost from their inception. He also told me years ago that his oldest son ridiculed an early computer that he considered archaic in design concept. Rocky said that he had invented it as a major technical advance for that day!

This book tackles the question of truth and how it affects our belief structures in both science and theology. Rocky has successfully bridged the gap between the ways in which we express truth in the different disciplines of knowledge. As he says it, "Truth is truth"; and he goes on to show how descriptions might appear different until examined closely. In a very rational way he presents the case for using reason to the point of acceptance or rejection, with faith buttressed by revelation as a final determinant for acceptance. I suggest you read the whole book of how a rocket scientist looked for God and then at God. For him, the tools of the Cyber Age have been a boon to forging new linkages between different segments of knowledge, leading more and more to a unified explanation of who and what we are and how we came to be. This undercurrent of logic and scientific developments provide the reason aspect that, together with faith, permeates acceptance of our religious beliefs.

Along the way, the reader will come to be informed about all the creation, growth, accomplishments, and future potential of our Cyber Age.

Cardinal William H. Keeler
Archbishop Emeritus of Baltimore

Preface

The genesis of this book was an exchange of e-mails with Father Patrick Heelan, S.J., a professor and fellow at the Woodstock Theological Center at Georgetown University and a past provost of the university. I met Fr. Heelan at a dinner I hosted at the University Club in Washington in the spring of 2005. It was to be a group of eight thinkers who would meet to discuss current problems of the day. By happenstance, Fr. Heelan sat on my right. I apologize to the person who was on my left, because Fr. Heelan and I engaged in a spirited discussion throughout the evening.

Rocket Ships and God was written for two reasons. First, in a selfish way perhaps, as a personal justification to myself that there is no gap between the truths of science and religion. Secondly, I wanted to share these findings with others.

Innumerable papers and books have been written about a supposed gap between science and religion. Nonsense! Truth is truth, no matter what the discipline. However, the description of a truth may vary widely according to the describer's language, jargon, and training. Also, many theologians freeze their intellects at the sight of an equation, no matter how simple; and scientists are often too deeply involved in a rigid process of discovery, discussion, and description to consider alternative methods of approach and presentation. The gap is within our methods, not with the truth.

I am a scientist and a student of philosophy and theology. All my adult life, I have wondered and pondered about God. Does God exist? Can we prove that existence? Can we establish some facts about the nature of God? Is there more than one God? In this book, I attempt to provide a logical basis for establishing answers to these questions based on fact, which should be acceptable even to unbelievers.

The question of the existence of God has been in the forefront of human thought since the beginning of history. There are hundreds of "proofs" for God's existence, and in these pages I attempt yet another proof that uses the findings of science. But only faith can fully bridge the gap from reasoning to acceptance.

The answers that I have proposed do not attempt to answer the how and the why of each phenomenon. My inability to understand how something works does not in any way diminish my ability to accept its workings as true. I do not know how an afterlife works but I can accept that it is true; nor do I know how electricity and light work, even though I know they exist and I know how to use them.

Science has no corner on the truth, despite what many modern pied pipers have claimed to a credulous public. It is true that scientific assertions are tested by a long, tedious process designed to be replicated and confirmed by other reliable scientists. But life is simpler than what pied pipers would have us believe. Often we know what is true even if we do not have the proof at hand. Common sense often precedes process and sometimes precludes it. One way or another, we will find truth. When we do, the sensible thing is to accept it, put your faith in it, and follow it.

Preface

Indeed, accept even what you cannot understand, so long as you know it is true. That's how scientists are forced to handle the mysteries of light, electricity, magnetism, and countless other cornerstones of the universe. The open secret is that no scientist yet understands many of the day-to-day phenomena that we all must accept about the universe. What they cannot fully explain, scientists learn to work with. If a thing is true—whether it is magnetism or the majesty of creation around us—why be hung up on *how* it is so? Of course, we continue to ponder and explore these mysteries and sometimes solve one or two. But do not, on science's account, stop using the truth because you cannot totally comprehend it!

We accept, live, and enjoy life. We were created to be happy. Our God-given hope tells us that full understanding will come later.

Rocco Leonard Martino
Villanova, Pennsylvania

Acknowledgments

No book of this nature can be completed without significant research and continual typing and retyping as the text is changed. I am indebted to my son, Joseph Martino, for his patience, energy, good humor, and never-say-die attitude, no matter how I changed wording, structure, and created, eliminated, and moved paragraphs. My sincerest thanks to Sister Joan Dugan, S.S.J., who was meticulous in smoothing my word flow and in checking my logic and clarity. My thanks also to Rebecca Brown and Patricia Popelack for retyping the final manuscript and Adrienne Holcombe for doing the final diagrams.

I wanted to be sure this was not an autobiography per se but rather a personal odyssey of my quest for truth and for God. I also offer my love and heartfelt thanks to my wife, Barbara, for tolerating my absentmindedness, silences, and long walks as I contemplated how to write of my strong belief that the truths of science and religion are completely compatible and never contradict each other; rather, it is people who speak in a babble of tongues who create division. I hope this book will point the way to correcting that problem.

I am grateful to Cardinal William Keeler for writing the foreword to this book. During our many years of friendship, we have often discussed these topics. It was a privilege to be able to tell him the conclusions of this book and to discuss with him the work of Bernard Lonergan, S.J., whom he knew as a teacher when he studied at the Gregorian University in Rome.

Much of the inspiration to write this book came from friends who were priests and nuns. I dedicate this book to them generally, and specifically to a number of priests and great Jesuit friends, all almost brothers. Specifically, I will name a few who stand out so clearly in my mind and heart, some still with us, and some smiling down at me as I type this:

Archbishop Joseph Pittau, S.J.; Bishop Alfred Jolson, S.J.; Father John Blewett, S.J.; Father Donald Clifford, S.J.; Father Patrick Heelan, S.J.; Father Milton E. Jordan; Father John Laboon, S.J.; Father Arturo Lozano, S.J.; Father Domenic Maruca, S.J.; Father Edward Nowlan, S.J.; Father Gerald O'Collins, S.J.; Father Stephen Pisano, S.J.; Father Nicholas Rashford, S.J.; Father Myron Delmar Skillingstad, S.J.; Father Michael J. Smith, S.J.; and Father John Snyder, S.J. They all evoke great memories over so many years: ice cream cones in Rome, pilgrimages at Lourdes, walking in the halls of the Gregorian University, duets with Barbara, sailing, Mass in the pool house, praying together, lunch in the kitchen, Mass around a table in our home, being anointed when all thought I was dying, marriages and baptisms of our children and grandchildren, comfort at funerals, and just plain basic friendship. I also wish to add Father Bernard Lonergan, S.J., whom I never met, but whom I admire and wish I had known in person and not just from his writings. And, of course, Cardinal Avery Dulles. S.J., whom I met many times but wished I had known much better than I did.

I am gratified at this opportunity to dedicate this book to them and to all priests and to all men and women "of the cloth.

Rocket Ships and God

1

Do We Need Faith to Build Cell Phones? (Yes.)

Faith is to believe what we do not see; and
the reward of this faith is to see what we believe.

—St. Augustine of Hippo

We often hear of "discoveries" that sound too good to be true. Or warnings from authoritative scientists that a catastrophe is about to end life on earth as we know it. It has also been revealed, based on the latest economic research and market behavior, that the entire world's financial system will collapse back to the Stone Age—*six months from now*. But how many times has the world ended? And how many times have other wild things been claimed (say, that we will soon be able to talk to animals, chatting over coffee with our family pets) that have not come to pass?

History is full of hoaxes, errors, lies, and deliberate misrepresentations designed to advance some purpose. The Bible even warns that we will see false prophets and prophecies as one sign of the approaching end of time (cf. Matt. 24:11). The Nazis under Adolf Hitler were famous for their Big Lie technique and used it to great effect. But potentates and politicians before and since have used much the same method. So have pressure groups

3

that have a cause to sell and money to make. For all these dis-
semblers, truth is relative—that is, what they tell you is related
to whatever they are trying to sell!

There are many definitions of relativism, but all of them concentrate on truth that depends on the situation, the person, or
the time. You have "your truth," and I have mine. For example,
a relativist might say that the concept of zero isn't objectively
real except insofar as someone believes in its usefulness. That is
rubbish. Some truths are absolute, and the concept of zero is one
of them. The existence of the universe is another. The fact that
there exist laws of nature whereby there is *order* in the universe
is obviously another.

On the other hand, the perception of countless shades of
green is genuinely relative, a matter of opinion or judgment
—only an interior decorator can see them all, right? But the
existence of the color green, which you can measure in a spec-
trometer, is a fact.

Trying to stretch the idea of relative *opinion* to obscure an
absolute *truth* is relativism. Pope Francis reminds us that there
is absolute truth—a truth that gives life and light. That is the
truth that *relativism* obscures, leaving confusion, darkness, and
ultimately, death. Pope St. John Paul II described the world created by relativists as a "culture of death." On April 18, 2005, this
same thought was at the heart of then-Cardinal Joseph Ratzinger's
homily to the cardinals as they were about to go into conclave.
Following is the essential, historic passage in which the world
first heard the phrase "dictatorship of relativism" (in the original
Italian, "*una dittatura del relativismo*"):

> Today, having a clear faith based on the Creed of the
> Church is often labeled as fundamentalism. Whereas

relativism, that is, letting oneself be tossed here and there, carried about by every wind of doctrine, seems the only attitude that can cope with modern times. We are building a *dictatorship of relativism* that does not recognize anything as definitive and whose ultimate goal consists solely of one's own ego and desires.

We, however, have a different goal: the Son of God, the true man. He is the measure of true humanism. An "adult" faith is not a faith that follows the trends of fashion and the latest novelty; a mature adult faith is deeply rooted in friendship with Christ. It is this friendship that opens us up to all that is good and gives us a criterion by which to distinguish the true from the false, and deceit from truth.[1]

The cardinals who listened to those words elected Cardinal Ratzinger pope — Pope Benedict XVI — the next day. Then in March 2013, the next pope, Francis, linked his own thought, his faith, and the direction of his pontificate, to Ratzinger's words:

It is the spiritual poverty of our time, which afflicts the so-called richer countries particularly seriously. It is what my much-loved predecessor, Benedict XVI, called the "tyranny of relativism," which makes everyone his own criterion and endangers the coexistence of peoples.... Francis of Assisi tells us we should work to build peace. But there is no true peace without truth! There cannot be true peace if everyone is his own criterion, if everyone

---

[1] Cardinal Joseph Ratzinger, homily to cardinals, April 18, 2005, http://www.vatican.va/gpII/documents/homily-pro-eligendo-pontifice_20050418_en.html.

can always claim exclusively his own rights, without at the same time caring for the good of others.[2]

What, How, and Why

How can we know the objective truth? Not all surprising claims are untrue. In science, many discoveries seem incredible until they are proven to be genuine. In religion, there are startling developments in theology, and such "unbelievable" events as miracles that are verified by outside experts. How do we judge?

There is a widespread belief that there is a built-in conflict between science and religion. But consider the parallels between them. The truths of science are established using a methodology developed over centuries by many brilliant minds in many places. This approach is loosely labeled the scientific method. It is used by scientists *and* theologians. Both types of thinker, pondering the questions of who we are, how we are, and *why* we are, follow a path of logical analysis based on prior accepted truths and more recent, but publicly verified, discoveries.

In the Catholic Church's investigations—whether she is investigating the cause of a saint or considering a theological or moral question—official inquiry follows a path similar to that of experimental science, using procedures and principles that can be replicated by others. The credentials of the examiners—whether they are specialists in that discipline or the general public—are a major factor in the evaluation process. Hence, the

[2] "Pope Francis to Diplomatic Corps: Church Fighting Poverty, Building Bridges," March 22, 2013, Vatican Radio, http://en.radiovaticana.va/storico/2013/03/22/pope_francis_to_diplomatic_corps_church_fighting_poverty%2C_buildin/en1-675745.

Do We Need Faith to Build Cell Phones? (Yes.)

process of discovery and authentication becomes the cornerstone in evaluating the credibility of the proposal, or of the *what*.

We will find that in both theology and secular science, the reliance on faith, truth, and standard methods of inquiry are essential. As we'll see later, they also arise from the same source: the intellectual and philosophical tradition of the Catholic Church. My hope is to create for our time a standard, unified method for establishing truth—whether the question is scientific or theological. I call the approach Unifying Theology and Science, or UTS. We will apply UTS to the fundamental tenets of Christianity, evaluating the truths in which Christians place their faith. UTS is the *how* to find *what* in order to answer *why*.

All examinations of phenomena, whether scientific or theological, are attempts to understand the present and predict the future. We will see that the methods of science and theology—including the scientific method, the Scholasticism of St. Thomas Aquinas and St. Albert the Great, dialectics, and the twentieth-century Jesuit Bernard Lonergan's Method in Theology[3]—are parallel approaches in a unified search for truth. Along the way, the supposed conflict between science and religion will be revealed as nonexistent.

Faith in the Cyber Age

This is the Cyber Age, when we hold the world in the palm of our hands—figuratively and literally. With the combined power of the computer, instant global communications, and wide-ranging visualization methods, we can see and be seen anywhere, hear and be heard anywhere, examine anything anywhere, and search

[3] See Bernard J. F. Lonergan, *Method in Theology* (Darton, Longman and Todd, 1972).

7

Rocket Ships and God

for facts of any kind at the touch of a finger. Individually, we have almost unlimited power to observe, communicate, and examine.

As I wrote decades ago before the fall of the Berlin Wall in 1989, iron curtains cannot stop electrons. Very little can be hidden from us forever. It is within our power to establish to our satisfaction what is true. In contrast to Karl Marx's vision of the helpless, manipulated masses, we are quite free to decide whether religious faith and ritual are only myths—"opiates for the people," as Marx called them—or a doorway opening to the mysterious and profound truth.

Religion is a set of rituals and beliefs directed to supplication, gratitude, and devotion to the supernatural. It is based on a faith in the significance of the future of each person, especially after death. Consciously or not, and whether or not you believe in God, your faith in your own significance—something that cannot be proven—is the rudder that provides purpose and direction in your life's voyage.

But in this Cyber Age of instant everything for anyone, is religious faith an anachronism? Do we need God when we have so much physical control over our environment and life? Or is religion an unnecessary burden to the progress of humanity?

This book represents the conclusions from my own search for the truth and my gut-wrenching look at my own future. To work out a system for evaluating claims to truth, my frame of reference is what I know. And what I know is mostly what I've learned in designing rockets and sending them into space.

Space travel demands precision—as close to perfection as possible. The results are based on exacting research that has revealed what physically works—which is the definition of the truth, as far as space travel is concerned. But interestingly, Walter Shirra, one of the original seven U.S. astronauts, is purported to have said as he shut down the engines three seconds before an early space blastoff, "It's tough sitting up there on top of all the lowest bids ... but you need faith."

What? *Faith?* Operating at the pinnacle of hard science and harder technology?

Shirra's comment described not a blind wish but the confidence, inspired by his knowledge of the system he had worked in for years, that others before him in the process had done their work diligently, investing their self-respect in his safety.

We're not going to get around the need for faith. To begin with, faith is not particular to religion. It is the glue that holds our thoughts together—assuring us that certain expected things will in fact occur. We are willing to ride in an airplane because we have faith in its design, faith in the skill of the pilot, and faith that the plane's systems of navigation and control will work. Most of our fellow passengers are not scientists; therefore, most of them are acting out of faith in a science they do not understand. Nor are scientists exempt from the daily need for faith. There are many fine scientists—generally not engineers—whose knowledge of how their own car starts is limited to where to insert the key and how to turn it. Yet they cheerfully drive to work every morning.

At the basic level, faith is a thought process, the confidence that lets us accept as true what we cannot fully determine by observation and measurement—and get on with the day. It provides the support to explore new ideas, to expand our range of experience and make discoveries without fear that the world won't work today more or less as it did yesterday.

Fear and Exploration

Religion has always been our search for a way to pierce the unknown, to go beyond the veil of death to discover our origin, the powers that move the world, and our destiny. From the dawn of history, we have wondered who we are, what we are, and why we are here. The ancient Greeks and Egyptians believed that each thing in the world was some combination of four basic elements—earth, air, fire, and water. They attributed the favorable or unfavorable events of their lives to various gods—whom they tried to appease or befriend for better results. On another channel of the Greek mind was a boundless curiosity and wonderment that led them to catalog and measure their world and try to discover the laws of nature, logic, and philosophy. These two channels of the human spirit represent what we call religion and science.

Can the truths of science and theology be unified into a single, cohesive collection of truth that can be universally accepted?

Here is the difficulty: the human mind can go only so far with its reasoning ability before it encounters a wall of unknowns. Those with a scientific, nonreligious point of view distrust what they see as emotion-driven, wishful thinking in religious speculation about the unknown. Yet to search the record of scientific calculation alone as a way to discover the truth is to discover, again and again the inadequacy of calculation alone to reveal the unknown.

The ancients were both curious about the universe and adept at measuring the movements of heavenly bodies. The initial presumption was that Earth was the center of the universe and that the sun revolved around it. These theories were reinforced by the most accurate numerical measurements that could be made at that time. Later it was proposed that the planets, including Earth, revolved around the sun, and that the sun was part of a larger universe with other stars. Once again, theories were developed and calculations were used to prove the validity of the premise.

Do We Need Faith to Build Cell Phones? (Yes.)

Which hypothesis was closer to the truth? We know now that the heliocentric (sun-centered) version is correct. But for centuries, the facts confirmed that the geocentric (Earth-centered) hypothesis was valid—because, using the data available, the geocentric model *worked*. It just wasn't true.

And what is light? In some experiments and applications, light acts as if it were composed of waves of energy. In other situations, it behaves exactly as if it were made of particles—we call them *photons*. In numerous other cases, both models apply. We know more or less what light does, but we can't be sure what it *is*, so we invented something called Quantum Theory to have it both ways.

And one more example: science and engineering have produced the cell phone with "smart" capabilities—it's almost a miracle of technology. Quantum Theory was required to do this, and yet we can't explain Quantum Theory itself. We have to accept the results and use on faith various parts of the theory, without understanding how they fit together—if they do.

In any field of knowledge, we will always encounter areas of mystery prone to doubt. With our reason, we consider alternatives, but uncertainty still prevails. We don't have all the information and never will. So we make the best judgment we can. The same is true in religion and science.

Many people accept the Big Bang Theory to explain the start of the universe. That is a leap of faith, since those who accept the theory weren't there to see the Big Bang. They're relying on the experience, sophistication, and calculations of others—who weren't there either. So that's two leaps.

Yet many of those same people cannot accept the notion of a Creator and the reasoning of popes and theologians. They argue that, unlike religion, science is real because it is rigorous and does not require faith for acceptance—although we have just shown that science does indeed require a certain faith. To such people, the rigor of science is sufficient to establish a chasm between the tangible *reality* of science and the unreasoning *faith* required to accept the tenets of religious belief. But unreasoning faith has not been absent from the development of science.

The central institution of faith in modern civilization, the Catholic Church, was the great catalyst to scientific development itself, as she fostered the preservation of knowledge through the Dark Ages and then served as the main launching platform for the study of science by founding and maintaining the first universities—at Paris (in 1000), Bologna (in 1088), and Oxford (in 1167), and one of the world's first astronomical observatories at the Vatican (in 1580).

Then there is the necessity of faith itself for scientific inquiry to keep going. We've mentioned that scientists can't say whether light is a wave or a particle. How can a scientist live with this obvious contradiction and return to work each day? We have faith that the development of Quantum Theory will solve this dilemma. Does this reliance on faith mean that our scientific theory of light is not rigorous? The mathematics is rigorous, and so we accept it. But this half-answer seems a little tenuous if the entire raison d'être of science is that it is rigorous.

The same conundrum applies to magnetism: we know how to use it and what it will do—but what is it? In fact, here we invent a mathematical element that does not exist. It is an *imaginary number*—the square root of minus one ($\sqrt{-1}$)—that we need in order to establish the laws for the behavior of magnetism and electrical circuits (German physicist Gustav Robert Kirchhoff's laws, to be precise).

A study of mathematics itself will show that the entire edifice of this rigorous language—which we use to describe phenomena in all scientific disciplines — rests on a foundation of seven basic axioms *that cannot be proven.* Fortunately, there's more to science than rigor.

Faith truly abounds in science! The fact is, many of the fundamental tenets of science are just mathematical models we derive to produce a "solution" that describes what we see or detect with our instruments. We have no certainty that we are describing the truth in its entirety or indeed that we fundamentally understand what is going on at all. Here are some other theories used in science that may or may not prove to be accurate:

- the ever-changing theory of subatomic particles, such as quarks, muons, gluons, neutrinos, and many more

- String Theory, which proposes the existence of multiple universes[4]

- a Unified Field Theory that will resolve all the puzzles mentioned, plus the rest of physics, ranging from falling apples to atomic bombs

Hence the most rigorous aspects of science often demand faith — or at times, the suspension of disbelief. Albert Einstein (1879–1955) commented, "As far as the laws of mathematics refer to reality, they are not certain; and as far as they are certain, they do not refer to reality."[5]

---

[4] String Theory postulates that subatomic particles are one-dimensional strings rather than points.

[5] Albert Einstein, *Sidelights on Relativity: I. Ether and relativity. II. Geometry and experience,* trans. G. B. Jeffery, D.Sc., and W. Perrett, Ph.D. (New York: E. P. Dutton, 1923), 28. This quotation is Einstein's answer to the question "How can it be that mathematics, being after all a product of human thought which is

Rocket Ships and God

Let's turn this question around. Rather than examining the ad hoc, faith-based aspects of scientific inquiry, can we mathematically describe a tenet of Christianity—say, the Trinity? Certainly. Consider a set containing three subsets, each of which in turn contains an infinite number of subsets. Each of the three subsets represents one of the Persons of the Trinity. And each of those three subsets contains all the attributes of one of the Persons of the Trinity. The subsets are equal. The set of three we call God.

Note that we could, if we chose, change our description of God. We could extend that entire set called God to include an infinite number of subsets. Hence, there could be an infinite number of persons in God. As with String Theory, there also could be an infinite number of universes for our God to rule. In other words, we could describe any situation with great *precision and objectivity*, following all the rules of mathematics, but it wouldn't in itself make any of our descriptions *true*.

This reality—that to be precise and wrong is to be precisely wrong—is often ignored in the popular media and in statements made by or attributed to scientists. The best teachers and communicators among scientists present a balance of their findings and theories and the statistical levels of confidence in any findings they present. For the greatest scientists, truth is more important than notoriety. But reporters are rarely so careful in describing scientific news. The amount of estimation, judgment, and error in the practice of real science would be a revelation to those who get their science only from the popular media—since a scientist, as he is usually presented there, is a quasi-religious figure, a modern oracle, and anything he utters has to be true.

---

independent of experience, is so admirably appropriate to the objects of reality?"

Do We Need Faith to Build Cell Phones? (Yes.)

Let's return for a moment to light. We know a lot about it, and it has always existed—we think. But, as we said, we invent a mathematical way to describe what it does, because we still aren't sure what it is. But lest the reader assume that nothing is what it seems to be, be assured that we can truly measure phenomena in a rigorous, mathematical fashion that is reproducible in other places and other times—for example, the speed of light. We know it is a constant and that nothing in the universe can be faster.

Oh, wait—that was then. Recently scientists found that a particle in physics, the neutrino, moves faster than light. In fact, there is now evidence that light in general is slowing down. There is also conjecture that the speed of light might have been almost infinite at the Big Bang.

For centuries, the speed of light was taken to be a constant. But early in the twentieth century, Albert Einstein proposed his Theory of Relativity to account for the apparent changes in the speed of light in the observations that Albert Michelson and Edward Morley encountered in the perihelion of Mercury during an eclipse in the 1900s. Einstein's general Theory of Relativity, published in 1905, said that the speed of light was constant in itself but varied according to his position of the observer measuring it.

Einstein's Theory of Relativity was widely accepted as a modern extension of Isaac Newton's Laws of Motion, as promulgated in the seventeenth century. Newton separated position and time; Einstein linked the two so that everything had a four-dimensional characteristic—three for space or position, plus one the dimension of time. Now, in the twenty-first century, there is a reexamination of whether to link space and time. If this new examination is accepted, space and time will be separated again, relativity will be out or demoted, and we will be back to Newton.

Rocket Ships and God

No matter how complex the mathematics, the essential fact remains that such things as Quantum Theory are not absolute. They are empirical attempts to create theory to match what we measure. Science, with all its precision, logic, experiment, observation, and rigorous proof, still requires a great deal of faith for people to accept basic premises and findings. Yet technology based on science does work! We can launch vehicles into space, create major networks of communication, build bridges that do not collapse, and predict the weather with increasing accuracy. In building bridges using modern physics, we have new confidence in the stress factors, equations, and load-bearing assumptions used. We have even added correction factors for temperature variations and vibration. With faith *developed from experience and reason*, we build new bridges with new designs over longer spans. The important element here is that the work of others leads a new engineer to have faith or confidence in the rules and laws of bridge design. Perhaps we should invert the phrase "faith and reason" to "reason and (then) faith"!

Back to theology. Earlier, we applied mathematics—set theory—to describe the Trinity. Let's do something more useful: let's apply the findings of science and the scientific method to the examination of a fundamental tenet of monotheism—the existence of a single Creator or God.

The title of the recent book *The Grand Design*[6] refers to the authors' belief that the universe spontaneously came into being out of nothing in 10^{-43} seconds. As an astrophysicist myself, I do not believe it. In other words, I do not accept on faith the authors' scientific premises or conclusions. My own premises

---

[6] Stephen Hawking and Leonard Mlodinow, *The Grand Design* (New York: Bantam, 2010).

point me in a different direction, and they happen to lead to an idea about God.

It is widely accepted that the projected age of the universe is about 13.7 billion years. Furthermore, it contains over 100 billion galaxies, each of which contains 200 billion stars of a wide variety. To date, we have found only a limited number of planets associated with some stars in the universe. The sun in our solar system is only one of the billions of stars in the Milky Way galaxy.

Now, it is possible to develop a probability that everything we know has occurred because of chance. The chance would be one in an infinitely large number, and therefore a pretty small chance. Since scientists have established through consistent measurements that the universe is expanding, the most likely scenario is that things evolved from some starting point over time, a very long time, to what we have today.

The expansion of the universe gives credibility to the Big Bang Theory. What existed before that instant in time? What set the whole thing going? What set the rules of evolution, chance, and control into effect? This is an unnatural or supernatural possibility that requires an unknown cause. Let us call that unknown the Creative Force. (We're allowed to do this. This is science. If we can describe the mystery of light as Quantum Theory, we can call this unknown source of order the Creative Force.)

The Creative Force by definition must have existed before time, energy, and matter existed. Nothing comes from nothing. Even if matter came from energy, the energy had to be created. So whatever created the energy field is the Creative Force. The Creative Force set into motion the rules of nature that we now have some inkling of. These are the laws of gravity, magnetism, energy, motion, et cetera. While in our brilliant yet finite minds we can begin to understand how each of these works, we have not yet pieced together the whole set into a single Unified Field Theory that covers all the natural phenomena. We believe it is so. There are many pointers to reinforce this belief.. Does a Creative Force exist? It is logical to assume so. Reason tells me that there is a Creative Force. Further reasoning, especially through the lens of String Theory, puts forth the premise that perhaps time existed before the Big Bang. That has been a theological argument for some time—that the Creative Force always was. Scientifically, we are learning more and more of the idea of curved time as well as curved space.

All of a sudden, the truth and premises of both theology and science are coming to the same conclusion. And why not? Truth is truth. Reason will allow us to identify certain characteristics of the Creative Force, or God, if you prefer, which we then accept on reason or faith—because it is proven, or because there is no better answer, or because we believe it is true.

A prime reason to believe the Creative Force exists, and is God, arises from the discovery of atomic energy. During the Second World War, Einstein wrote a letter to President Franklin Roosevelt suggesting that an unstable uranium mass—for example, uranium 235—could be exploded and converted into energy; and that energy would have a devastating effect as a bomb. The Nuclear Age was born on August 6, 1945, when an atomic bomb was dropped on Hiroshima, Japan.

Calculations were based on an equation developed by Einstein in 1905, which came as a byproduct of his general work on relativity. This is the very famous equation that created the bomb: $e = mc^2$—that is, energy equals mass multiplied by the speed of light squared. With nuclear bombs and nuclear power, it is the conversion of mass into energy that is important. The equation also indicates that mass may be created *from* energy.

Do We Need Faith to Build Cell Phones? (Yes.)

We can develop the relationship that follows from the first as night follows day: $m = e/c^2$

Let's put this equation together with the Big Bang, which is commonly accepted even by atheists. A very large mass exploded to create the universe. It happened in an infinitesimal part of a second — 10^{-43} seconds, to be exact. Where did the mass come from? Assume it came from energy. Hence a quasi-infinite energy field created a vast amount of mass, which exploded. That quasi-infinite energy field we can call God.

To connect the dots, the quasi-infinite energy field referred to as God created the mass (our universe) that has been expanding ever since. As a result, the existence of a supernatural Creator is *not* contrary to the tenets of our modern concepts of science, especially of physics and astronomy. You might even say it's a necessary explanation!

This example interjects scientific considerations into valid questions associated with religion. And why not? It simply extends the use of scientific formulas to handle data in a new arena, which is why we create these formulas in the first place. Truth is truth and is valid in all branches of knowledge.

In the usual theological and philosophical sense, we are accustomed to think of the attributes of God as that of a loving, caring, and protective supernatural being. We as the creatures of this all-powerful God consider ourselves to be made in His image. Is our personal sense of God contrary to the image I've just presented of God as an infinite source of energy with the power to create the universe? I believe there is no contradiction between those attributes, as I hope to make clear.

Faith, or confidence in a proposed process or fact, is something that applies as a factor equally in any branch of knowledge and, in fact, in life as a whole. We have faith that the pilot of an aircraft is competent; we have faith that people will stop at a red light as we proceed on green; we have faith that experimental observations presented as valid can be duplicated by others; and we have faith that the sun will rise tomorrow morning and set tomorrow night. That faith is based on other sets of knowledge and confidence in the truth of what we have to believe or accept.

Yet we often accept the basic truths of science, and new findings, with a kind of natural skepticism. Judgment is needed in striking a balance between justified scientific faith and skepticism. For example, when testing by the European Organization for Nuclear Research (CERN) results showing that the speed of the neutrino apparently exceeded the speed of light, there was much skepticism as to the accuracy of the experiments, despite the careful analysis and reputations of the CERN scientists. When the testing was duplicated, the results were the same, and much, but not all, of the disbelief evaporated. A wait-and-see attitude prevails. This is healthy. If these results are true, new theories are necessary. Even then, however, these theories will not affect how light is part of our lives and of the universe. Studying its properties systematically can give us a greater understanding of what it is. But what it does is, and has been, known.

So there it is. Faith is an element in both science and religion — and in life. Faith leads to exceptions beyond what can be reasoned or proven by experiment or observation. It is used as a final step in the process of discerning truth. There is no conflict between the truth of any discipline of knowledge, since truth is truth. Faith and reason (or better, reason and faith) in the Cyber Age is buttressed by the findings in many disciplines of truth. The love of the Creator for us, the creatures, becomes readily apparent as we delve deeper and deeper into the mystique of the beauty of nature and the phenomena of mankind.

2

Reality versus Truth:
How Do We Know What We Know?

The truth will make you free.

—John 8:32

Truth is an *invariant*. Even if it is twisted, incorrectly described, misunderstood, or unknown, it doesn't change. It's still there and still true. Imagine drawing a circle on a sheet of rubber. The sheet may be twisted in many ways, even into a pretzel. And yet the basic figure on the sheet *is* a circle, regardless of how it appears to us as the sheet is twisted. In mathematics, this is the Theory of Topology, or the study of invariant figures. Like truth, the circle we've drawn is an invariant.

Now, here it gets a little weird. Reality is not the same thing as truth. Reality is a phenomenon—something we perceive. It's very consistent and reliable. But it's still subjective and therefore may not be *true*. Why not? Our senses or our interpretation of what our senses tell us might have it wrong—just as we can't easily see that what's drawn on that twisted sheet of rubber truly is a circle. And since it's an interpretation, it can change—it's not invariant.

Rocket Ships and God

Everything true is real—but not everything *real* is *true*. For instance, a mirage that is created when the sun's rays are bent by a temperature inversion in the desert air can reflect the image of an actual oasis that is miles from the spot where you "see" it. The mirage is real—anyone in your place would see what you see. And the oasis does exist. It just isn't where it appears to be. So, while the mirage is *real*, it is not also *true*.

Bear in mind that whatever is true in one field of knowledge is true in all disciplines—since truth is invariant. Truth in science is an element in the set of all truths. Similarly, a truth in philosophy, theology, or logic is equally an element in that same set—the body of truth. Here are some logical ground rules describing the set of all truths:

- All elements of truth are equally true.

- No element in the body of truth can be in conflict with any other element, since all are true. If there appears to be a conflict, either one of the elements is not really true, or we are mistaken in seeing a conflict.

- A premise being verified as true can be tested by any method, so long as the procedures can be repeated by others.

- Such procedures can be solely cerebral (mental) or can include physical observations or measurements or logical inference based on other truths.

- Something known only by revelation can also be an element in the body of truth. Truth is independent of us. Hence, it does not depend on how we come to know it, if we *do* come to know it.

- Truth—being invariant—is immutable.

Reality versus Truth

But . . . What Is Truth?

In his book *As Bread That Is Broken*, nuclear physicist Peter van Breemen, S.J., begins chapter 3, "Free in Truth," with the following:

> The word "emeth" is a Hebrew word which, until recently, was considered synonymous with the Latin word "veritas" (truth) and is now translated "fidelitas" (fidelity). It communicates a knowledge of God. It is for the Hebrew an existential word. His life, his whole existence is rooted in the fidelity of Yahweh. He can trust Yahweh. Yahweh will never let him down. That's "emeth". To Westerners, truth is something intellectual. Truth means that the idea and the word correspond to reality. This is less profound than the eastern meaning of the word. John, in his Gospel, uses the word many times; e.g., "the truth will make you free" (John 8:32). We miss the whole point if we interpret truth in this context as meaning *intellectual* truth. The truth John speaks of is this: the reliability of God's love. . . . "Emeth" is the noun, and the corresponding verb is "aman"—to confirm. Our "amen" stems from the same verb. God says "amen" to my existence, and he will not go back on His word.
>
> I really do matter to God.[7]

As a scientist, I search for the truth; as a thinking man, I *think* I can handle it. But I often think of Jack Nicholson's character's retort to Tom Cruise's character in the movie *A Few Good Men*: "You can't handle the truth." Searching for truth is not easy. And

[7] Peter G. van Breeman, S.J., *As Bread That Is Broken* (Denville, NJ: Dimension Books, 1974).

what is less appreciated is that it often takes determination to *accept* the truth once you find it. What qualifies a thing to be accepted as truth?

Introducing Science and Religion

We have different avenues of perception by which we accept something as true. One is, of course, what we see with our eyes, in the everyday sense. If you see someone steal a car, you tend to accept your perception of the act as true. But what about things we can't see but we know are true—such as the abstract *fact* that the sun will come up tomorrow or that man is mortal? In human history, two of the fundamental avenues for knowledge of what we might call "invisible truths" have been religious belief and, later, science.

As discussed in the previous chapter, men have always been inspired by their fear of the unknown. In many cultures, they envisioned the forces of nature as individual gods and developed guidelines for their own behavior to avoid the wrath of the gods and even to achieve happiness of one kind or another in an afterlife. In this way, religion came to embody a code of beliefs and behavior that regulated conduct as well as offering the comfort of a relationship between a people and their God or gods.

On a parallel path, using the same human minds, men have sought knowledge and truth by looking into the heavens with the idea of *measuring what they perceived*. The ancient Greeks meticulously mapped the movements of the constellations in the *galaxea* ("milky circle" or Milky Way) around them and tracked the looping paths of the *planetes asteres* ("wandering stars" or planets) that they saw in the night sky. In the modern era, we still carry on the Greeks' project in visual and electronic explorations of the universe. We use such tools as the Hubble

Space Telescope with its eight-foot optical mirror, peering into space and time from its orbit high above the earth—avoiding the distortion of the truth caused by looking at heavenly bodies through the lens of gases in our atmosphere. After our simple space flights to the moon and to a manned space station, we are poised to travel to other planets and perhaps even farther, as our science develops more complete knowledge of the universe and the relationships between space and time.

Our ancestors' search for the truth was later informed by Church teaching that *God loves us*. One of the implications of this idea is that because He loves us, He has created *an orderly world that can be discovered and understood by us*. He encourages us to discover and understand this world, because He wants us to know Him better. These two philosophical-theological ideas ultimately created what we call the scientific method. The essential tools of that method—called the three legs of the scientific method, on which discoveries of scientific truth depend to this day—are not inherently high tech or even material in nature. They are powers of the human mind: intuition, observation, and measurement.

Contrasting the Scientific and Theological Methods

Theology, the detailed study and justification of religious belief, is often referred to as a science, having existed for centuries before the birth of modern experimental science. Although both are highly cerebral, with conclusions based essentially on products of the mind, there are significant differences between them. Science is dominated by the scientific method. For a thousand years, theological and religious development utilized the Socratic method, essentially analysis advanced by dialogue, in which premises are disputed until agreement is reached. In the Middle Ages, this was supplanted by the Scholastic method—made famous in the thirteenth century by St. Albert the Great and St. Thomas Aquinas—whereby elements of the truth are established one by one based on what is already known or can be proven by logic.

Different ways of knowing involve different ground rules regarding what constitutes "admissible evidence" of the truth. Consider for a moment a physicist and a poet explaining a sunset. Do you think their descriptions would be the same? The physicist might say, "I am facing west at the end of the day. The sky at the horizon exhibits a range of colors with a predominance of red. The color in the sky is caused by the scattering of the light photons as they collide with dust particles in the air. The gradual disappearance of the sun confirms the earth's rotation from west to east, and that the next sunrise will be in the east as the earth's rotation continues. It is a striking view."

The poet might concentrate on aesthetics and on the impact on the psyche, linking the beauty of the sunset to an elevation of the spirit: "At the end of the day, the sky is suffused with rays of red and gold, lifting the soul. The panorama is breathtaking. The sun makes its rapid descent, a fiery ball quenched into darkness as it falls below the horizon, but in death continues to recall its glory by the color it splashes on the sky where it has been. Thank You, Lord, for this beauty, this day. It will begin again with the rising of the sun, calling to mind Your glory and power. Good night, dear Lord, with our humble thanks for making our world beautiful.

These descriptions are very different. And yet the sunset was absolute—real—a single, true event. So what is true, and how do we determine what is really true? In fact, how do we go about even finding out what the choices are?

Briefly, truth can be absolute (objective) or relative (an experience particular to a point of view), or a blend of the two.

Reality versus Truth

Perceiving the truth often requires some language or method of transmission, even to clarify our own thoughts to ourselves. But as something independent of us, truth does not require description by us in order to be true. One implication of this is that there could be beings who know things directly—this is how angels and their intelligence are often described. For such beings, description is not necessary. They do not have to make their way to the truth; they are already "there."

The Scholastic method includes a great deal of objective reasoning and observation. The scientific method relies heavily on subjective intuition and evaluation procedures of the results derived in an objective manner. Not surprisingly, subjective and objective considerations are essential aspects in both.

Absolute and Relative Truth

If you set out to buy white paint for your living room, you will quickly discover that you have to choose which shade of white you want. A lawyer friend once told me that there are over two hundred such shades. Hence, it is easy to see why there is so much concern with what is true and what is not. There are spinmasters who will "prove" to you that white is black. When you reluctantly agree after a long harangue, they will then prove you are wrong and show that white is really gray. And yet the color is white, although the exact shade will depend on the interpretation of the observer. So it is with the concepts of absolute truth and relative truth.

Absolute truth is what *is*—as opposed to the mere reality that appears consistently to the senses and mind of an observer, which could be mistaken. Absolute truth measures and includes *more* than reality, since many things are true that we are not aware of. For example, we are not really aware of the truth about black holes, although we know they exist. The nature of black holes and the laws that regulate them are unknown. But black holes are part of the body of truth. The truth of what is really happening in and around them is not yet determined, assimilated, or accepted by us. It may never be.

As we pointed out, reality is a subset of truth. Supernatural phenomena such as divine visitations or intercessions on earth are also true, but may not be real—that is, they may not be among the things we can experience or comprehend.

Descriptions of sunsets may be quite different, but the absolute truth of the sunset remains valid. In the example of the physicist and the poet, the sunset was observable—apparently clouds hadn't obscured it. But even if it had been invisible to any observer, it would have been true.

Looking at a sunset, you might say it is brilliant, short, and breathtaking. You might say that the closer to the earth's equator the observer happens to be, the shorter the sunset is (and indeed, sunsets at the equator appear to be very sudden, compared with elsewhere). One sunset can appear longer than another *to an observer*—when atmospheric conditions disperse the light in such a way as to provide a longer twilight than would occur in other locations with a clear sky.

But sunsets are *in truth* absolutely identical everywhere: They occur when a given point on the surface of a planet rotates beyond the tangent of the sun's rays and ceases to be struck by any of those rays. The variation in how sunsets *appear* to someone does not change what they *are*. All that changes is the cognitive realization (the sensory and mind experience) of the sunset *in the observer*.

If a sunset is described with absolute scientific terminology with regard to the variations of date and time, such data can be analyzed, examined, and experienced anywhere at any time. On the other hand, in subjective interpretation, one sunset is not necessarily capable of being duplicated by others. Much of its *phenomenological* reality is subjective.

The seventy thousand people who witnessed the sun crashing toward Earth at Fátima, Portugal, on October 13, 1917, experienced such a phenomenological reality.[8] From an astronomical point of view, the sun did not suddenly dive toward the earth. There are some who would ask whether this was a case of mass hysteria. But it is hard to believe that seventy thousand people would be subject to mass hysteria.

Absolute truth does not tell us everything that is real. For instance, the sun effect at Fátima was real. Truth defines only what *is*, irrespective of an observer's experience.

Truth Exists and Sometimes Laughs at Us

There are many today who will tell us very earnestly that there is no such thing as absolute truth. They claim that all truth is subjective and relative — that the observer's experience is all.

"Fine," you say obligingly. "I accept that you're right. I'll agree that it's absolutely, reliably, objectively *true* that all truth is relative ... Oops! Wait ..." You stop yourself apologetically. "It seems I've uttered a contradiction! If it's absolutely *true* that there's no absolute truth, then that would be an instance of a truth that *isn't* relative. Your statement can't be true, because that would make it untrue ... if you see what I mean. So you're wrong. Sorry!"

When you think about it, we must accept that there is both absolute truth and relative truth. We can take the earth itself

---

[8] Many witnessed this phenomenon during an apparition of Our Lady of Fátima to three shepherd children.

as an example of how there can be absolute truth and relative truth with regard to the very same phenomenon. To us, the earth seems bumpy and full of potholes. We're told it's spherical, but it seems like a pretty sloppy copy of a sphere. For instance, it's a bad idea to go for a stroll near the edge of the Grand Canyon wearing a blindfold—one false step could mean a six-mile drop to the bottom. And think about it: the highest point on Earth is Mount Everest, which is 29,029 feet high—more than five miles above sea level! And the deepest part of the sea is the Marianas Trench, approximately 36,200 feet deep—more than six miles *below* sea level!

From those measurements, let's agree in round numbers that the earth's greatest divergence from being a perfect sphere is eight miles or less in any one instance. Let's see: the earth has a diameter of eight thousand miles. That means that, as a sphere, it's off by less than one *thousandth* of its diameter. If the earth were reduced to the size of a standard tennis ball (about 2.65 inches in diameter), then that tennis-ball-size earth would be perfectly spherical to a tolerance of less than *four ten-thousandths* of an inch. We cannot manufacture anything that smooth. We can say that, *absolutely* speaking, the earth is a sphere.

But we would still watch our footing when walking near the Grand Canyon.

Phenomenological Reality

Here is one of the most concise statements I've read about what reality is and what it is not: "Reality is that which, when you stop believing in it, doesn't go away."[9]

---

[9] Philip K. Dick, in his 1978 speech "How to Build a Universe That Doesn't Fall Apart Two Days Later."

Reality versus Truth

Software engineers have created computer programs that we call "virtual reality." They can build a program that allows us to walk within a house that does not exist. We can see paintings on the wall, climb stairs, and even see people moving about within it. But it's not there. We can put on a glove and shake hands with a person anywhere—who might not exist. We can see group pictures showing people who weren't there when the photograph was taken. We can hold a meeting on our computer screen that looks like a regular boardroom meeting—but actually, everyone you see on the screen sitting around the table together (including yourself) is logging in from a different location.

The concept of virtual reality is not new. It is present in the use of perspective in the drawings and paintings of the Renaissance masters of the sixteenth and seventeenth centuries. There are church ceilings in Rome that those masters painted that appear to be domed—but in truth, they're flat. These masters could even paint portraits in which the eyes of the image appear to follow you as you walk back and forth in front of them. Virtual reality is *not* just a modern computer phenomenon.

On a similar scale, there have been great advances in creating artificial intelligence, often associated with computer technology, but not solely so. Although these logical and mathematical approaches can simulate a form of conversational or logical reality, they are strictly techniques created by the mind of man. Artificial intelligence (AI) can never be used to reason, to create intuitively, or to determine right from wrong. Rules can be programmed into the system, but the device can never work beyond the patterns written into it. Robots are a special case of AI, often manipulated and controlled by a person.

And here's one that isn't about computers: religious visions are real to the participant, but not necessarily to witnesses or spectators (although, as at Fátima, they sometimes *are* visible to spectators).

Schizophrenia has often been defined as being out of touch with reality. The schizophrenic lives in different worlds, each populated with different persons and situations. Only one of these worlds is real. The hallucinations may include real people and events; or they may contain people and events that exist only in the mind of the schizophrenic.

Perceptual differences can cause variation in the reality an observer experiences. If we have two observers and one of them is color-blind, there is a chance that estimations of color as reported by the observers will differ. In fact, the same differences exist among people with normal color perception. You and I say that something is blue. Are we seeing the same thing? Color for each person is a cognitive interpretation of the information his senses provide him with. There is no guarantee that the visual systems in your brain and mine see the color in exactly the same way. Just as we create different virtual realities in a computer-generated program, we must assume that there are differing aspects of reality in our respective brains.

We could say that because *all* reality is interpreted through thought, all reality is virtual, and truth alone is factual. Therefore, in describing truth and reality, it is essential to include all the conditions under which observations are made — in such a fashion that they can be duplicated or experienced by others in different places at different times.

As I proceeded in my studies in the Scholastic method and Thomistic philosophy on one hand, and the scientific method on the other, I was chagrined at the lack of attention to method and absolute documentation in philosophy — whereas such care is a prerequisite in science. I might add that as I delved further into science, I found unbelievable inconsistencies not only in science, but in the bedrock of mathematics, which is supposed to be the foundation of science.

Is Reality Just Probability?

In science, reality is what can be measured in such a way as to be repeatable by others for verification. But science is not as neat or clear-cut as many people assume.

As we noted in chapter 1, one of the great difficulties for centuries in science has been the difference of opinions as to whether light is a particle or a wave. Quantum mechanics was invented in the early twentieth century to explain and include full sets of observations — regardless of whether they supported the particle model or the wave model. We say that there is a probabilistic or oscillating pattern or rule that permits light to act as a particle or a wave, depending on the circumstances. We accept that it acts in two ways, even though we don't yet understand why.

One common way of describing this duality is to consider the toss of a coin. A coin toss can come up heads or tails, but not both. Similarly, even though light photons can be waves or particles, a particular photon can't be both at the same time.

Let's think about probability for a minute. It sounds vague. But such a "vague" calculation of probability can be closer to the truth than a hundred events happening in front of your face. For instance, chances are equal that, if you toss a coin, it will land head up or tails up. If there are millions of coin tosses, undoubtedly it will be proven that half are heads and half are tails.

But note that if you make only three coin tosses, it cannot be said that half will come up heads and half tails. As a matter of fact, you may get *three heads and no tails*. So, even though a 50-50 probability means that there is an equal chance of a head or a tail, that doesn't guarantee that heads and tails will come up an equal number of times in a given series of coin tosses. It's even conceivable that there could be a string of nine heads coming up before tails comes up even once. But that occasional oddity does not change the probability—which is a truth—of 50-50 for every coin toss.

Similarly, there is no guarantee as to whether these or those photons in a light example will exhibit either wave or particle intensity.

The Basics of Life around Us

Whether it is by the scientific method, the philosophic method, the Scholastic method, the Socratic method, or the method of dialectics, we are searching for what is true. We all have our own preconceived viewpoints, our own jargon, our own experiences, and our own set of beliefs. And yet—truth is truth. No matter how we describe it, a sunrise is a sunrise, a child is a child, and life is what we all live until our bodies and minds no longer live.

All of us will agree that the memory of each life resides in the minds of others. Some of us also believe we will still live after our minds and bodies have ceased to do so—that such memories live on in us in what we call our souls. In short, some believe in the supernatural, and some do not. Some accept the existence of God according to the great mathematician and philosopher Blaise Pascal's philosophical "wager." Pascal advanced the argument that you should accept belief in God, since at the very least, you have nothing to lose by doing so: if you believe and comport yourself accordingly during your lifetime, and God's heaven turns out to be real—you win. On the other hand, if you accept God's existence and grace as true, and they are not, you have lost nothing. So you might as well believe and accept. That is Pascal's wager: heads, you win; tails, you do not lose.

In contrast, some insist that religious faith is an absurd delusion because truth is only that which can be seen, heard, or touched. And yet the same people operate on blind faith—without visual, auditory, or tactile evidence—that sunset will occur this evening, as it did yesterday evening. And if the predicted time of sunset occurs when the sky is cloudy, rendering the sun invisible, they will still accept that the sun indeed set. With a similar faith, many militant atheists readily accept the existence of atoms, viruses, and even subatomic particles—which they cannot see and probably never will.

In the Internet Age, when information is immediately available to anyone, anywhere, at any time, we now see an intense, widespread inquiry about the interface between science and religion. The theme has become topical with school boards around the country, and there is a resurgence of interest in evolution. Students of all ages and interested adults have become aware of the claims and counterclaims of adherents to various philosophies and denominations. Before our eyes, there is a popular search for truth. There are, of course, a lot of bad answers being turned up in addition to the good ones. But the search is a healthy thing.

3

Religion, Theology, and Science:
The Many Arts of Seeking Truth

There is a common belief that science and religion are incompatible. Usually when people say this, they mean that it is religion that must go. Yet science, even in the modern era—with all our scientists, technology, and results—has never factually proven religious truth to be in error. Some scientists and intellectuals have criticized the idea of faith, but for reasons that I hope are becoming clear, they cannot prove it wrong: faith is a necessary part of all inquiry, including scientific inquiry.

Simpleminded antireligionists today go so far as to suggest that we discard religious belief in favor of belief in something they call science. The problem is that real science is not a religion and does not consist of a disdainful attitude toward people or ideas of the past. Real science, in fact, has no content. It's simply a method—called the scientific method—and a commitment to the truth. What happens is that sometimes the spirit of open, scientific inquiry collides with the faith of those in authority.

At times, Church authorities have challenged scientific inquiry as being disruptive to an orderly society, and some scientists over the centuries have had their work sidelined or suppressed.

Rocket Ships and God

The most well-known, of course, is Galileo (1564–1642), one of the most brilliant scientific minds who has ever lived. He proved that light objects are pulled just as strongly by gravitation as more massive ones. He improved the recently invented telescope and discovered craters on the moon, spots on the sun, the fact that not all celestial objects orbit the earth (he found moons orbiting Jupiter), and the fact that there are vast numbers of stars invisible to the naked eye. With others of his period, he changed reality. Galileo also argued in favor of the heliocentric (sun-centered) model of the solar system published by Copernicus seventy-five years earlier—which said that the earth went around the sun, and not the sun around the earth. That, and his irascible personality got him into trouble. The personal, the political, and the circumstantial often prove crucial where cultural values collide.

Nicolaus Copernicus (1473–1543) was a canon lawyer of the Catholic Church, an astronomer, a medical doctor, an economist, a military strategist, a poet, a diplomat, and an all-around genius from Poland born ninety years before Galileo. During Copernicus's life, Pope Clement VII and several of his cardinals listened with great enthusiasm to lectures on his new theory of our solar system. One of the Roman cardinals wrote Copernicus to praise his research and ask him to send copies of his published works.

But a century later, heliocentrism was still not generally accepted among scientists, the Church, or the Protestant reformers. It went against everyday experience and against respected theories of the ancient Greeks; it even seemed to contradict certain phrases in the Bible. And as a hypothesis, it wasn't proven: The measurements that would demonstrate that the earth was orbiting the sun could not be made until new advances in telescopes made them possible in 1838. The heliocentric theory was, however, true.

Copernicanism, as it was called in the seventeenth century, was being written about openly but cautiously as an unproven hypothesis — which in fact it was. Galileo's career might have ended better if he hadn't mocked his friend and protector, Pope Urban VIII, by portraying him as a foolish opponent of heliocentrism in a satirical book on the subject called *Dialogues*. And it might have helped if Galileo had been content to publish his opinions on the subject as working hypotheses, as the Vatican's Holy Office had already approved, rather than as absolute truth. In 1633, the Inquisition charged Galileo with violating the terms of its approval of his book. They sentenced him to abjure publicly the Copernican system and to live (comfortably) under house arrest in Siena, where he continued his research and writing until his death in 1642.

In 1979, Pope John Paul II ordered Galileo's case reopened. In an address before the Pontifical Academy of Sciences in 1992, the pope reported the panel's findings exonerating Galileo and saying that Church authorities had erred in forcing him to recant his views.

After the 1917 Revolution in Russia, "Scientific Atheism" became the state religion, and it soon came into conflict with actual science. The Communist Party took control of research, education, and commerce. Protecting the party's power, rather than discovering the truth, was made the goal of science. There were some scientific theories that one could not criticize unless he wanted to go to prison; these included the work of Trofim Lysenko (1898–1976), a plant biologist and agricultural administrator whose theories were considered important to Soviet Communist rule. Lysenko rejected the theories of the

Rocket Ships and God

Moravian monk Gregor Mendel (1822–1884), the founder of genetics. Lysenko's research (falsely) claimed not only that treating winter wheat plants with moisture and cold air made them hardier against Russia's harsh winters but also that the toughening effect on those plants *changed their DNA* and was successfully inherited by wheat grown from their seed, resulting in bountiful harvests.

Lysenko's theories and claims were valuable to Stalin and the Communist Party because (1) they promised to show that the Soviet takeover of family farms could produce bountiful harvests instead of starvation; and (2) they could suggest that there is no fixed human nature, and therefore the Soviet takeover of industry and society could mold and manage human nature to be obedient and successful for the sake of the state—instead of causing bankruptcy and poverty.

None of it worked. We know what happened in the end. By 1990, seventy years of trying to suppress the truth had led to the collapse of the Soviet Union and most of the vassal governments it had created in Eastern Europe and around the world.

Objectivity does not come easily to us. We can't breathe in the truth or intuit it like the angels. So we need tools to gain *knowledge*—views of the truth from this or that angle. Plato described knowledge as something "justified through belief." But the scientific side of our brains recognizes that if we want to get to the truth, we need objective facts, rather than facts as we would wish them to be.

The disciplines of science gather, filter, and codify some of the elements of the set of mankind's *total knowledge*. Each discipline stakes out its own point of view and maintains its own body of facts, discoveries, and logical analyses it has accepted as valid and important. Each discipline also has its methods for seeking evidence, refining information, and discovering error—and its own hall of scientific heroes and villains.

How we acquire ideas depends on the unique traits of the people acquiring them: what they're curious about, how they think, what they believe, what else they know, and what their personal obsessions and enthusiasms are. Before we can call people's ideas "knowledge," we need to cultivate the ideas objectively and determine whether they are true. Always, we must remind ourselves that scientists' motivation for contributing raw ideas to the world is as subjective, varied, personal, emotional, artistic, partisan, ambitious, vindictive, noble, or holy as the individual scientists themselves.

Philosophy and Theology as Sciences

Let's look at some of the tools we have for deciding whether ideas qualify as scientific knowledge. These are, of course, tools of the human mind.

Philosophy describes the behavior of the human mind and spirit and their relation to the world. *Theology* seeks to understand the nature of God and the relationship of the human to the supernatural. Both philosophy and theology are considered to be sciences—distinct from each other yet obviously intertwined.

What we now call science itself was referred to by Aristotle as *natural philosophy*. Like philosophy and, later, theology, it began with the mental exercises of reasoning, using *passive* observation of phenomena and deliberations about them. One of the most striking examples is Newton's inspiration about gravity as he observed a falling apple.

What followed was the *active* pursuit of discovery through deliberate experiments. The alchemists were the forerunners of chemistry; German astronomer Johannes Kepler (1571–1630),

Copernicus, and Galileo were the pioneers of experimental physics.

The development of mathematical method began at the same time. The universe, wrote Galileo, "cannot be understood unless one first learns to comprehend the language and read the letters in which it is composed. It is written in the language of mathematics." Mathematics became the language of logical analysis in science, consolidating observations and experimental results into theorems and laws. Theology arose from logical analysis of Scripture, the Church Fathers, Tradition, and observations of the behavior of the human spirit.

Logic is one of the most hard-edged tests of critical thinking. Its purpose is to establish how we know what we know. It offers us two ways of coming to a conclusion and supporting it:

1. *Inductive* reasoning draws its conclusions from specific examples.

2. *Deductive* reasoning draws logical and general conclusions from ideas and their consequences.

A classic example of inductive reasoning is the theory we've described defining the nature of light—which can behave as a wave one moment and a particle the next. It is *inductive* reasoning—from observation, measurement, and calculation—that led to Quantum Theory. To get our practical engineering work done in the physical world, we accept the reality that light can behave in either fashion—without (for now) needing to understand how this is possible.

An example of *deductive* reasoning is the set of geometric theorems developed by the Greek mathematician Euclid (c. 300 B.C.), who also created the system of logic that followed from them. The most familiar geometric theorem is the Pythagorean theorem, which states that in a triangle containing a 90-degree angle, the sums of the squares of the two shorter sides equals the square of the length of the third side (called the hypotenuse). Like inductive reasoning, deductive reasoning requires a suspension of disbelief, a leap of faith, in order to proceed—but it is a *different* leap from the inductive one. Rather than forcing us to make do with contradictory observations without seeing the big picture, deductive reasoning paints a very complete picture for us indeed, where seven axioms lay the foundation for conclusions that follow from them with perfect, satisfying consistency. But here is deductive reasoning's leap of faith: those seven axioms must simply be assumed at the start. They can't themselves be proven.

As a discipline, logic is generally agreed to have begun with Aristotle. He drew a distinction similar to the one between inductive and deductive reasoning: he referred to *analysis* and *synthesis*. Analysis takes an object of study and examines its component parts. Synthesis considers how the parts can be combined to form a whole.

Informal logic is the study of arguments using everyday language. The study of incorrect paths is an especially important part of such studies—that is, to identify the true path by showing how the others lead to error or absurdity. Plato made generous use of this technique. So did such giants of the Scholastics as St. Albert the Great and St. Thomas Aquinas in the thirteenth and fourteenth centuries.

Formal logic uses deductive reasoning and reaches its conclusions through the form, rather than the content, of the statements being proved or disproved. Also called *symbolic* logic and closely related to *mathematical* logic, it's the branch of philosophy you'll see using symbols to indicate relationships between statements and ideas, such as an arrow for *implies* and a triangle of dots to indicate *therefore*—and a great many other symbols. Many of the symbols are the same ones used in algebra.

Boolean Logic

Boolean logic is an extension of symbolic logic, devised in the mid-nineteenth century by an English cobbler's son and self-taught mathematical genius, George Boole (1815–1864). This logical system is central to the operation of today's computer systems. It is a binary algebraic system and is used primarily in circuit switches database searches. This system instructs a computer's operating system using *or, not, and,* and *xor* (exclusive *or*), combining search terms to limit or expand the numbers of results.

The power of Boolean logic is its simplicity: it lets us use the most basic forms of expression to represent any logical possibility. For example, if you are interested in finding all papers associated with vaccines developed specifically for lymphoma cancer, your search might read: "Search for research AND lymphoma cancer AND vaccines." If the search is to be limited to papers written in 2009, then the search statement would be something like the preceding with the addition of "AND 2009."

Now let's say you want to narrow your search to research conducted at the University of Pennsylvania in Philadelphia. In that case, the statement would read as follows: "Search for research AND lymphoma cancer AND vaccines AND 2009 AND University of Pennsylvania."

Boole's work is often referred to as "the algebra of logic," a description immortalized by Ernst Schröder, who produced a work in three massive volumes on Boolean logic and algebra called *The Algebra Logic.*

Religion, Theology, and Science

Methods of Analysis

The ancients had no Google or Internet. They had only one research tool—their minds. Nor was it possible for thoughts and ideas to be easily shared with others over a distance. Knowledge was shared personally, often through conversations in a circle of thinkers whose propositions were advanced or disputed by their fellows. The earliest formalized approach that we know of was in the time of Socrates, whose famous student Plato described his master's methods. The tone and range of inquiry in such philosophical circles may be hinted at by the title of Plato's famous philosophical book on love and human nature, *Symposium*—ancient Greek for "drinking party"—where Socrates figures as a participant. Plato had an equally famous student himself: Aristotle. In the Socratic method, participants might be friends, other teachers, students, onlookers, or a mix. This dialectic technique of conversational "academies" continued through the centuries.

In Hebrew culture, similar academies were built around the Temple. Toward the end of the first millennium, Catholic monastics and scholars refined the Socratic approach of challenging questions and answers into a written format that came to be called the Scholastic method. In the thirteenth century, St. Albert the Great became its foremost exponent, surpassed only by his brilliant student St. Thomas Aquinas.

The essence of Scholasticism is (1) clear delineation of the respective domains of philosophy and theology and (2) the use of reason. In religious matters, Scholasticism advanced various premises taken from Scripture or as presented by revelation in the tradition and dogma of the Catholic Church. Counterarguments to every point within were presented and stripped away, allowing the premise to be considered true. From the beginning, Christian thinkers were confronted with this question: How are we to reconcile reason with revelation, science with faith, philosophy with theology? Although philosophy relies on reason alone, theology uses the truths derived from revelation. There are also some truths—the mysteries of faith that are completely outside the domain of philosophy—that belong to theology. The question is how to use *derived* truth and *revealed* truth to arrive at *complete* truth.

In the Scholastic domain with the Christian scholars, God is considered the author of all truth; hence, it is impossible to think that He would create a natural order that contradicts what He teaches in the supernatural order.

St. Thomas took as his task to examine all aspects of philosophy and faith, consciously carrying on the work of Aristotle —whom he refers to as the Philosopher—and influenced by many other thinkers, including Averroës (1126–1198), the Islamic Aristotle scholar from Cordoba in Spain, then occupied by the Moors—whom St. Thomas calls the Commentator. (For his persistent studies of non-Islamic manuscripts and philosophy, Averroës was eventually exiled to Morocco by Islamic authorities and died in the largely Jewish village of Lucena. His manuscripts were publicly burned.)

St. Thomas took on the task of examining all aspects of theological belief in the light of sacred documents and opinions dating back centuries. The work of such giants as Aristotle and Augustine were included in his analysis of each point of dogma. In St. Thomas's crowning achievement, the massive *Summa Theologica*, he examines the nature of God, the angels, the human soul, conscience, the virtues and vices, good and evil, and the afterlife.

Religion, Theology, and Science

Syllogisms

It was Aristotle who developed what is called *syllogistic* logic. A syllogism reasons from the general to the specific. The classic approach consists of three statements: a *major premise*; a *minor premise*; and a *conclusion*. For example:

If: All human beings are mortal (major premise).

And: I am a human being (minor premise).

Then: I am mortal (conclusion).

That works. But suppose we make the minor premise: "I am mortal." Can the conclusion "THEN: I am a human being" be correct? No. There are many creatures that are mortal that are *not* human beings. That is one of the problems with syllogisms. Here's another syllogism:

If: Men are human.

And: Women are human.

Then: Men are women.

You can see that this conclusion *can't* be correct—yet it looks fine in symbolic logic.

If: A = C

And: B = C

Then: A = B.

The problem arises if you equate the word *is* and the mathematical equals sign (=)—which denotes *two-way* equivalence. That leads to error because it overlooks cases where not all members of a given category also share membership in another category.

So we must be very careful how the syllogism is formulated. A landmark paper by German philosopher and mathematician Gotlob Frege (1848–1925), founder of modern logic, initiated an ambitious program to use more precise notation that would help in the rigorous development of mathematics. Although he focused almost entirely in the realm of natural numbers, he also discussed possible applications to geometry, analysis, mechanics, physics of motion, and philosophy.

Another example:

Water flows.

Blood flows.

Hence, blood and water both flow.

But "Blood is water" would be an incorrect conclusion.

From experimentation, we know that blood contains water, but to claim that this conclusion can be drawn from the syllogism is wrong. However, it can be argued that the fact that blood contains water is what permits it to flow. This sets up separate arguments and studies meant to investigate the statement "Everything that flows probably has water in it."

Although the limitations of syllogisms lead to obvious errors, that very fact confers a benefit: the errors are obvious. The process demands that we isolate all our assumptions—which is critical to arriving at the truth. Suppose you have an experimental result. How can you tell what caused it, as opposed to a phenomenon that merely occurred previous to it? Setting up the possible syllogisms points out the pitfalls and possibilities that can lead to the true answer.

Cyber Age Scholastic Methods

In science, the objective is to create and document laws of the behavior of matter that are reproducible by anyone, anywhere. Using mathematical descriptions strips away the mystery and the associations of words, allowing for complete understanding by anyone. Acceptance or rejection of a statement can be immediate.

Religion, Theology, and Science

This is not always possible in religion and theology. We often encounter situations in which reason cannot provide an answer. St. Anselm, a member of philosophy's A-team—along with Augustine and Aquinas—described theology as *fides quaerens intellectum*—"faith seeking understanding."

With faith in hand, it is vital to question and to define the situations where we have no answers. That is when the real work begins. There are only two possible reasons for not having answers: incomplete searches or incomplete knowledge.

In our Cyber Age, searches are relatively simple, and communication of results is easy. (Historically, this was not so.) But what about our knowledge? Is it too incomplete for us to make up our minds?

Most of the details of our religious belief are based on ancient and sacred documents. Are we satisfied with the facts of our accepted religious truth? While the earliest writings are more oracular than scientific, we know from archaeological, linguistic, and historical research that the Old Testament is a fairly good historical record based on the observations of mostly contemporaneous witnesses over a period of centuries. The New Testament Gospels were written quite close to the lifetime of Christ from accounts of those who had witnessed the events described. In addition, it has been established further that the Pauline epistles of the New Testament were actually written mainly by Paul. Yet, despite all this research, despite centuries of studies and discernment of brilliant scholars, much remains incomplete.

Dialectics

Dialectics is a method of argument that has been central in both Eastern and Western philosophy since ancient times. While it might be claimed to have originated with Socrates and extended

Rocket Ships and God

by Plato in the Socratic dialogues, dialectics is rooted in the ordinary practice between two or more people who have different ideas and wish to persuade each other. This was essentially the method used throughout history in Hebrew schools examining the teachings in the twenty-four books of the *Tanakh* (an acronym in Hebrew for *teaching, prophets,* and *writings*), which Christians describe as the Old Testament. The minimal foundation of any dialectical exchange is that the participants, even if they do not agree, must share at least some meanings and principles of inference.

In addition to the Socratic, Hebraic, and Thomistic forms of dialectic reasoning, you'll find an analogous commentary-and-response approach almost anywhere you turn, from the Hindu and Chinese philosophical traditions, to modern quasi-prophetic treatments of the writings of Georg Wilhelm Friedrich Hegel and Karl Marx. Briefly stated, two or more people orally debate a premise; or perhaps one person lists and addresses various possible objections to the premise himself—as St. Thomas did—and then applies reason to demolish the objections, leading to verification of the initial premise.

We can use dialectics to embark on an adventure: to turn to the supernatural as an adjunct to the truths developed from our cerebral examinations of history, of the world as we have seen it, of facts related to us by others (especially as related in manuscripts and books), and verbal lore, including legends. We establish to our own satisfaction and comfort what *is* true, what we *believe* is true, and what we *hope* is true. This is the halfway realm of believers, agnostics, and atheists.

In my own youth, I questioned a great deal. I found no answers and got little comfort for my questioning. I never quite made it to atheism, but during a certain period, I was only a few steps short of that. What is startling to me in hindsight is that I never felt abandoned by God. Rather, I was troubled because I drew no comfort from my search through ideas I had been taught from birth to accept. Still, I was fortunate. I did not suffer the spiritual depression of the kind we read about in the writings of Mother Teresa, St. John of the Cross, or Teresa of Ávila. Mother Teresa wrote that, prior to becoming a nun and for some time afterward, she felt very close to God and in full communication. And then the curtain dropped. She was plagued by desolation throughout the later years of her life. In the book *Mother Teresa: Come Be My Light*, she describes in letters sent mainly to her spiritual advisers how she felt ignored by God:

> This terrible sense of loss—this untold darkness—this loneliness, this continual longing for God—which gives me that pain deep down in my heart—Darkness is such that I really do not see—neither with my mind nor with my reason—the place of God in my soul is blank.... I just hear my heart cry out— "My God" and nothing else comes—The torture and pain I can't explain.

This "dark night of the soul," to use a phrase from the mystic St. John of the Cross, did not hinder Mother Teresa from her unity with Christ or from bringing the solace and comfort of Christ to the dying. Likewise, St. Francis of Assisi, St. Paul, and even St. Peter prevailed even though they doubted and questioned at times.

The writings of many mystics throughout history attest to the fact that they found truth and were satisfied that the truth would sustain them. Although comfort was their goal, they persisted even when their comfort was incomplete. Spiritually, they had traveled a good distance up the curve toward perfection even while, psychologically, they were at a point at which they felt abandoned. Rather than despair, they took this as a spur to work harder, to seek harder, and to become closer to God. So let it be with us. There need not be a magic bell that rings when we hit goodness or truth. It is a lifelong quest to find truth, to accept it, and to follow it.

In 1990, Father Gerald O'Collins, S.J., in the Jesuit magazine *America*, wrote of three theologies: the theology of the mind, the theology of the heart, and the theology of the spirit. He likened the theology of the mind to the cerebral approach taken in the United States, in Canada, and in Europe. Through this theology, through faith and reason, proofs for the existence of God and proofs for truth were revealed or determined.

The theology of the spirit is characteristic of the East, where awe, reverence, and holy fear prevail as man regards the power and majesty of God the all-knowing and all-powerful One who regulates all things. In this theology, the spirit speaks and eliminates doubt through faith and the stirring of the spirit.

I well remember the first time I attended Mass in the Eastern rite. It was at the Russicum, the Church of the Russian Catholic Church beside the Orientale, the part of the Gregorian University in Rome dedicated to the study of Eastern rites. I wondered why the Consecration was behind a screen, hidden from the faithful. I thought it strange until I learned that it was part of the mystery of the Consecration. The incense was heavy, leading to a certain heady feeling, intensifying a great sense of mystery and awe. The reverence of the faithful was in striking contrast to the almost casual demeanor we see in the pews in the United States and in Canada.

The theology of the heart is paramount in Central and South America, where Jesus mystically is felt laboring side by side with

His people. The heart leads the way to truth, to acceptance, and to dedication. I have watched pilgrims at the shrine at Guadalupe in Mexico City walk for miles on their knees, bleeding and torn. I marveled at their faith, appreciated it, but knew that in my cerebral conditioning I could never follow this path. I wished I could.

What happened for me is that, as a young man, Jesus was my buddy and my friend. As I grew, He grew and became the Jesus of the Passion and the Jesus of the Resurrection. However, as I aged, the Holy Spirit came to be a greater and greater factor in my life. I have often felt the presence of the Holy Spirit, even though I think of God the Father in the same terms as I think of my own father. For me, the Trinity is real.

There was a time, however, in my early twenties when, like Mother Teresa, I felt bereft of the presence of God and came to doubt. My cerebral approach left gaping holes and questions with no answers. But at least my cerebral approach was directed in the hope of finding truth.

My faith was challenged, crippled a bit, but never totally lost. I believed, but ... Was there *really* a God? Was there an afterlife? Do we have souls? Was Christ both God and man? How? Why? How could I tell? I read extensively — in a hurry, blessed by the fact that I had learned at a younger age to read rapidly. I learned that I was far from unique. My concerns and questions had been shared by many throughout history.

My Personal Quest

I began to study the nature of truth and how we came to accept the truths we hold when I entered the University of Toronto as an undergraduate in 1947. This came after two historic calamities of the twentieth century — the Great Depression and the

Second World War. For many, it was a time of rebuilding, of recreating a life of expectation. For the many returning veterans who had lived through terrible experiences, it was a no-nonsense time. While the churches were full and the laity were faithful, still there was skepticism. This state of mind affected many like me who had served as cadets but had never been near a battlefield.

I was especially concerned with what I saw as a "Take it or leave it" attitude in the Catholic Church. Dogma was presented to be accepted! I was a skeptic: How did all this happen? I was a caveman looking around the world, trying to figure out what it was all about.

I was deeply involved in my studies in mathematics and physics. Whenever I questioned such phenomena as the true nature of light, I was told by my professors that we really did not know the answer. I accepted that as a challenge, not as a failure or weakness in science. In Quantum mechanics, we were trying to patch together an explanation for why light was either a particle or a wave but not both at the same time. I was allowed to take any course I wanted at the university so long as I wrote the examinations in mathematics and physics. So I got to study St. Thomas and his works with some of the world's leading experts on the subject. I understood and accepted many of the conclusions in Thomism, buttressed by the writings and philosophy of St. Augustine and others.

Bernard Lonergan

I learned many years later that my peregrinations were shared by an illustrious fellow Canadian, the Jesuit Father Bernard Lonergan (1904–1984), who taught theology at the Gregorian University in Rome for many years. He was trained in science,

economics, the philosophy of history, and theology and was an
expert in Thomism. He produced a book titled *Insights*, which
challenged Thomism dramatically. His following book, *Method in
Theology*, presented his idea for a Generalized Empirical Method
(GEM) to study theology in a way equivalent to the scientific
method.

The basis of the Scholastic method is to test the documents
accepted by the Church against contrary views in order to establish their validity. Lonergan's doctoral dissertation modified the
Scholastic method with insights from the evolution of thought
and perception. In this way, he sought to integrate Thomistic
thought with the history, science, and philosophy of his day.

In *Insights*, Lonergan based his work on two prevailing questions about the human mind: "What is happening when we are
knowing?" and "What is known when that is happening?" By
focusing on knowing rather than on the known, Lonergan based
his work on *insight versus intuition* in science.

Level of Operations	Mediating Phase	Mediated Phase
	Analysis ↓	Deduction ↑
Experiencing	RESEARCH	COMMUNICATIONS
Understanding	INTERPRETATION	SYSTEMATICS
Judging	HISTORY	DOCTRINES
Deciding	DIALECTIC	FOUNDATIONS

Table 1: Lonergan's Functional Specialties

Rocket Ships and God

In his *Method in Theology*, Lonergan added a fourth level of knowing whereby the mind deliberates and decides. He divided theological questions into two phases. The first phase includes research, interpretation, history, and dialectic. The second phase encompasses communications, systematics, doctrines, and foundations.

The Fallacy of Dependence on Inconclusive Definitions

This will build on our discussion about that "leap of faith" required in geometry: Some things cannot be defined within themselves. They exist only in relation to something else. To prove this, consider figure 3.1. In geometry, it's an axiom that two lines intersect in a point. Another axiom states that a line joins two points.

What is going on in the case below? Being completely rigorous in our geometry, we could say that we have a point joining two lines:

—•—

or a line connecting two points:

•—•

Which is it?

It can be either, but not both. The definition of each element depends on our definition of the others.

These concepts of *line* and *point* are two of the seven axioms in mathematics, on which all of mathematics rests. Yet, following the logic of the axioms, a given line and point cannot be uniquely defined without reference to the other. In other words, at a certain level, the seven defining axioms of geometry don't successfully define a line or a point.

Religion, Theology, and Science

Let's go back to the idea of parallelism. We can say that two lines are parallel if they never meet, or if they meet at a zero angle, or if they meet at infinity. Those conditions sound as if they describe the same result. They do not. And here is one implication of that fact: Depending on which definition is used for parallelism, mathematically we can use it to prove that the sum of the angles of a triangle is either equal to, greater than, or less than 180 degrees. But that can't be! Using the axioms of geometry, we can prove that the sum of the angles of a triangle is always exactly 180 degrees.

So what is the truth? Each of those statements is true, depending on the frame of reference.

Back to the real world. If we use physical entities, things we see and handle, then we are correct in using our commonsense perceptions of lines, points, and parallelism. The rules of our senses, experience, and everyday logic are designed for usefulness and accuracy in our everyday lives.

On the other hand, to create an analytical tool using mathematics, we can define anything however we want and use the resultant logic to derive answers to questions we pose—where the answers depend on the rules. These answers can be totally foreign to our everyday experiences, our senses, and our observations.

Theories of science are based on assumptions meant to explain observations. These rules are often expressed in mathematical form—rigorous mathematically and, one hopes, scientifically. But they are only tools. They are not necessarily an expression of truth. So the answers may not make sense to us humanly, even though, for the purposes of the concepts we have created and the rules that go with them, they are correct.

The following examples will help drive the point home.

Rocket Ships and God

The Problem of Infinity and Unity

Mathematics is a language that can be used to describe phenomena—seen and unseen—real or not. Like all languages, there are nuances of meanings and tricks that can be played. One such example is what we mean by infinity. We can define it mathematically, but it can lead to conflicts when applied to everyday reality. This is important, since we use the idea of infinity in relation to the afterlife and to the existence of God.

What is *infinity*? Let us relate the concept to a *unit*, or one.

When we consider the number one, we think of unity, a single entity. If we take another single entity, we think of them together as making two—the sum of one and one. That is what we learned to recite as children.

As a child, I learned to say, "Two!" when my parents held up two fingers. When I was a senior in college mathematics, I learned to say, "It all depends." One and one could equal one; one minus one could equal one; and one could equal two. After I earned my doctorate and had my first job, I learned that one and one were whatever the boss wanted them to be. And when I asked young children what one and one was, they would look for the puzzle and ask warily, "Eleven?"

Things are not always what they seem to be or what we have "known" them to be.

Take a piece of paper and a pencil and draw a line one unit long. The unit can be an inch, a foot, or whatever you want it to be. This is called a *directed line segment of length 1*, regardless of whether we're talking about inches, feet, meters, miles, or what have you.

Take a strong magnifying glass and look at the pencil line. You will see a series of spots, because pencils leave gaps between the graphite transfers to the paper. Even if you use pen and ink, what appears to be a solid line will show up under magnification as a field of spots. Mathematically, we say that the directed line segment is composed of a *very large number* of spots. If you use a digital camera, you will find that the line has a few million pixels, or points of color. As a matter of fact, because when we draw the line we are spreading individual molecules of pigment, we say the number can be larger than the largest number we can imagine. This we call an infinite number. Hence, we can say physically and materially—not simply by abstract definition—that the unit line segment is composed of an infinite number of points.

With that under our belts, let's try a simple subtraction problem: From this infinite set of points, remove an infinite set of points. In other words, we now have one minus one (1 − 1). What is left? Why one, of course—an infinite set of points. *Really?* Yes, it works, because we have defined this as an infinite set of points: since this is an infinite set, beside every point I remove there must still be points on each side. This is handled by the Heine Borel Covering Theorem (fig. 3.1):

An infinite set of points

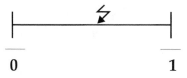

0   **1**

Figure 3.1: The Covering Theorem

We have a directed line segment of length 1 consisting of an infinity of points. Take away an infinity of points, or a line segment equal to 1, and an infinity of points remains, since, in infinity, for every point removed, there are points on each side that remain.

Hence we have: 1 − 1 = 1

Got that?

Now, another mathematical stunt: take an equilateral triangle—i.e., a triangle whose sides are all equal and whose interior angles are all equal. The angles are each 60 degrees, but that is not a factor.

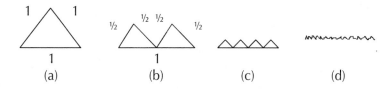

(a)   (b)   (c)   (d)

Figure 3.2: An Equilateral Triangle

As shown in figure 3.2a, the sum of the lengths of the two upper sides is 2 (1 + 1). The length along the bottom is 1. Now, as in figure 3.2b, divide the triangle into two triangles. The upper sides now comprise four half-unit lengths—which still add up to 2 units, while the bottom is still 1. Next, keep dividing the top again and again, millions and millions of times, until the triangles become dots, as in figure 3.2c. Keep dividing an infinite number of times (figure 3.2d). Since the upper sides now comprise an infinite series of dots that are becoming infinitely small, the number along the upper sides is approaching 1, and we can call it 1. Limit theory tells us we can do this. And since the dots are becoming infinitely small, we can define them as points. And if we do, those points form a line with a length of 1. So in the end, 1 + 1 = 1.

To summarize:

$1 - 1 = 1$ (figure 3.1)

$1 + 1 = 1$ (figure 3.2)

Hence, $1 - 1 = 1 + 1$

Or, $0 = 2$

This is all valid mathematics.

It simply shows that mathematical rigor can be misleading if you try to equate mathematical concepts with reality. Mathematics can create its own reality based on its own rules and come up with a mathematically correct absurdity.

These examples merely point (as it were!) to the fact that mathematical concepts are simply tools for describing different aspects of the truth—not the truth itself—which is why the tools sometimes clank against each other and produce absurd results. The truth is something out there, which science shows us parts of, one part at a time.

Science is not the whole truth; sometimes it's not even the truth at all. It's also not one thing. It's lots of measurements and concepts that add up to a small part of what we sense or understand is the universe.

Science, in other words, is a thing in God's universe—not the other way around.

Hermeneutics and Science

Hermeneutics is a term normally applied to the branch of theology that deals with exegesis—the interpretation of text. Among biblical scholars of the various denominations and religions, there seems to be little difference in their interpretation of the meaning of the words in ancient texts. Where the disagreement often comes is in whether the facts or assertions expressed by the words are true.

Rocket Ships and God

But Martin Heidegger (1889–1976), a member of the philosophical movement called hermeneutic phenomenology, argued that all description is always already an interpretation—that every form of human awareness is interpretative. The idea in hermeneutic phenomenology is to consider the equivalence of descriptions of a phenomenon no matter how it is expressed, whether as an algebraic equation, a vision, a poem, a painting, a legend, or a combination of all of them. For example, I read a doctoral research paper by Rola Ajjawi at the University of Sydney on how experienced practitioners learn to communicate clinical reasoning. As you might expect, each of the doctors presented to his readers, colleagues, or students differently from the way the other doctors in the survey did, even when the disease and treatment were directed in the same fashion.

The Input of the Describer

But the most important distinction between the branches of inquiry is between the ways they pursue their goals. Joseph Ratzinger, later Pope Benedict XVI, stated in his book *Jesus of Nazareth*:

> Religions do not aim merely to answer the question about our provenance; all religions try in one way or another to lift the veil of the future. They seem important precisely because they impart knowledge about what is to come, and so show man the path he has to take to avoid coming to grief. This explains why practically all religions have developed ways of looking into the future.[10]

[10]Pope Benedict XVI, *Jesus of Nazareth* (San Francisco: Ignatius Press, 2008), 2.

Religion, Theology, and Science

In its own way, science also attempts to see the future. Perhaps Aristotle's description of science as natural philosophy is the most fitting. Science is not totally the realm of stinks, sparks, and explosions. It is a methodology of questioning, observing, correlating, deducting, and concluding. Why does the sun rise? What are eclipses? Is Earth round or flat? What is light? How did all this come to be?

Objectives of Inquiry

Scientifically measurable truth progresses incrementally (at best). A sunset was known as an element of truth by cavemen. But it is only since Isaac Newton, who analyzed the dispersion of light into its constituent wavelengths, providing different colors, coupled with our knowledge of astronomy, that we have gained a wider understanding of the truth of a sunset.

In the sixteenth century, at the same time Copernicus was measuring the heavens analytically and discovering the true order of the solar system, Aztec rulers an ocean away, acting out of both religious fear and astronomical calculation, looked up to the same sun and sacrificed hundreds of thousands of innocent young lives every year, hoping to leverage supernatural power for their own survival and advantage.

In Christian culture, science and theology have developed different languages. When truth is examined scientifically, it is usually described through the use of the scientific method, with equations and mathematical nomenclature. Technical jargon can be a tiresome attempt to describe truth—although the rigor of technical precision is critical to allowing any scientist anywhere to understand exactly what the investigator has achieved.

All religions rely to some degree on what Catholics call "private revelation"—things known or experienced by individuals in direct communication with supernatural forces — which scientists in the lab might call "irreproducible results." Judaism and Christianity in particular address our personal relationship with God — and therefore use vernacular, idiomatic language. Jesus spoke a specific language to His followers: Aramaic. When He spoke to His Father, He often called Him *Abba* — Aramaic, not merely for "father," but a more intimate meaning akin to "Papa."

Unfortunately, an understanding of what is intended can be clouded by the nuances of the word used. This particular problem occurred in the creation of the many international translations of the new *Catechism of the Catholic Church*.

Beginning in the Renaissance, and continuing throughout subsequent history, science has progressed to the degree that it is a major factor in intellectual pursuits today. The number of practicing scientists far surpasses in significant multiples the total number of theologians and philosophers in the world throughout history — and also surpasses the number of scientists who lived before our time.

I strongly urge theologians and philosophers to embrace knowledge of science as a necessary requisite in their own endeavors. By the same token, I think it is vital to have scientists learn at least the rudimentary aspects of philosophical reasoning. While on the board of various universities, I always strove to increase the liberal arts content of academic programs, especially those in science and engineering.

For all the precision and order necessary in analyzing phenomena scientifically, human vision is limited, even using the powerful instruments available today. Therefore, the pursuit of any kind of truth is necessarily a *creative* endeavor. Freewheeling intuition is crucial in the formulation of hypotheses leading

Religion, Theology, and Science

to the theories and laws that explain the nature of our universe. And here, seeking the revelation of the imagination, it operates in the same realm as literature, art, and religion.

In religion, theology is the repository of the results of inspiration, observation, and analysis of nature, with particular attention to phenomena identified as outside of nature—that is to say, the supernatural. Most especially, these explanations include how everything started. Although science postulates the theory of the Big Bang, it is theology that postulates how matter came to be *before* the Big Bang. Darwin proposed a theory of evolution, whereas theology proposes the concept of intelligent creation and rejects chance alone as the source of life and creation. Religion is the application of theology to life and to our objective in living.

Truth is reproducible. That is, in a given set of circumstances, the event to occur is predictable. The sun rises, and the hour and minute can be found by calculation since the variations are predictable. If water is boiled at sea level, it reaches 212 degrees Fahrenheit or 100 degrees Centigrade when it begins to boil off, or evaporate. Those predictions are expressed in mathematical symbolism that is universally understood.

In Scripture, which is a form of religious truth, even an atheist can attest to the translation of a scriptural segment. However, when it comes to the meaning or interpretation of the words, there can be chasms of differences. And yet the truth is itself immutable.

People die. For some, they are reborn; for others, it is all over. What is the truth of death and life that awaits all of us? As Pope Benedict XVI said, religion's task is to pierce that veil of the future in our search for God. Our faith also tells us that the search is not one sided.

Rocket Ships and God

"Behold," Christ says in Revelation 3:20, "I stand at the door and knock." Do we answer the knock? Or are we sometimes hiding on our own side of the veil?

The poet Francis Thompson tells us that despite our evasions—perhaps because of so much that we do not wish to know about ourselves—the Hound of Heaven pursues us all:

> I fled Him, down the nights and down the days;
> I fled Him, down the arches of the years;
> I fled Him, down the labyrinthine ways
> Of my own mind; and in the mist of tears
> I hid from Him, and under running laughter.[11]

[11]Francis Thompson, "The Hound of Heaven," lines 1–5.

4

The Scientific Method in Perspective

The history of science predates the birth of Christ. Systematic geniuses in Greece — such as Euclid, Pythagoras, Socrates, Plato, and Aristotle — set the stage for the development of the scientific method. The first step is detached thinking about some mystery of interest; the next stage is experimentation, observation, and the organization of results; when successful, that leads to the discerning of patterns and laws that predict and explain behavior in the physical and natural world. Because it is a process of reasoning about the natural world, science was known as *natural philosophy* — Aristotle's term for it — well into the twentieth century.

Such is the order present in the universe that the existence of natural laws or truths created by God can be discovered by mere human beings like us. Not only that; the scientists who seek these laws don't have to travel to a mountaintop in Tibet or consult an oracle at Delphi. If we know how to look, we can see the laws of the Creator written in every atom and light beam.

So powerful are these laws — these secrets hidden in plain sight — that scientific investigators in the last two centuries have in some cases been able to use them to *predict what would later be discovered.* For instance, the planet Neptune was sighted through a telescope by Johann Gottfried Galle of Germany on the night of

Rocket Ships and God

September 23, 1846 and into the early morning of the 24th. The discovery had been predicted by French astronomer Urbain Le Verrier. According to Le Verrier's calculations, the planet Uranus wasn't following the orbital path predicted for it by Newtonian mechanics. The disturbance in its orbit was so strong, he reasoned it had to be caused by some unknown planet near it. But at that time, Le Verrier couldn't interest astronomers in France in looking for a planet at his coordinates. So he sent the calculations to Galle at the Berlin Observatory. Galle got to work the night he got Le Verrier's post and sighted the planet in less than an hour—within one degree of the position Le Verrier had specified.

As François Arago, head of the Paris Observatory, put it, it was actually Le Verrier who saw Neptune first—"at the point of his pen." ("Monsieur Le Verrier vit le nouvel astre au bout de sa plume.")

In a similar way, Pluto was discovered in 1930 by Clyde Tombaugh at the Lowell Observatory in Arizona after calculations by American astronomers Percival Lowell and William Pickering in Boston had predicted its existence as early as 1909.

Should we think of this ability to predict discoveries as God's gift to us—that He occasionally lets us look over His shoulder as He is driving?

The Philosophy of Science

We normally think of science as a field of experiment and observation. A critical branch of science does not involve experiments, however, but rather, observation, reasoning, and logic about how to practice science. This is the *philosophy of science*. The field focuses on science's "support beams," including its assumptions, methods, intellectual foundations, and ethics. Its practitioners include both philosophers and scientists. The job of the philosophy of science is to guide the logical and physical methods of science to ensure that they lead toward the truth. The scientific method is not limited to what can be seen, felt, or heard. Science is an *iterative* (repeating) method for applying conjecture, observation, and deduction to answer a question—where the process can be rerun with different variables until the question is resolved. A successful conclusion proves a truth through a sequence of steps that can be reliably duplicated by other investigators with the same result. For example, water will boil at the same temperature—varying in a predictable way with the atmospheric pressure—no matter where we are. Hence, we call that temperature (at the given pressure) *the boiling point of water*. It is a single "finding" that can be verified by anyone, anywhere, at any time.

Why Science?

Science is objective; that is to say, it is not associated with the mental or physical attributes of any individual scientist. Philosophy and theology, on the other hand, are heavily subjective, exploiting the intuition and experience of the philosopher or theologian. That is not to say that intuition is not a necessary factor in scientific discovery. Acting on a hunch based on experience in order to come up with a hypothesis that can be tested by experiment—that's typical in science. But intuition cannot prove the validity or even the meaning of a discovery. That must be confirmed by mathematical reasoning and experimental procedure, such that another investigator can follow the same steps to get the same result.

The scientific method is not the truth, but one method of uncovering it. And do not assume that it is immune from attempts to distort or conceal the truth. Whether the right answer emerges depends on whether the right question is being asked. If you are at thirty thousand feet, the boiling point of water you record will be a much lower temperature than the one you record at sea level, because atmospheric pressure decreases as altitude increases. Hence, if your experiment predicts and confirms that the boiling point of water is variable—but fails to include differences in the altitude of the samples for which you recorded the boiling points—your conclusion is worthless. The best measurement is only as good as the reasoning and wisdom that make use of it.

Should we consider science the be-all and end-all? Is it a curiosity of the intellectual or is it a factor in everyday life? Can science tell us about the nature and origin of life or point the way to the purpose of life?

Science, philosophy, and theology vary, not in logic, but in the type of knowledge they analyze and how it is discovered, verified, and accepted. Consider the interpretation of a passage in an ancient biblical manuscript: through science, scholars may agree on what the text says. But through the discipline of theology, its importance lies in what it demands of us through our belief or behavior. The reasoning is interpretive, rather than objective. At the same time, its end is more existentially critical. Through one discipline, we decipher; through the other, we act.

What comes to mind is the statement in *The Imitation of Christ* by German theologian Thomas à Kempis (1380–1471): "A humble knowledge of oneself is a surer road to God than a deep searching of the sciences." But in his very next sentence, he reaffirms his respect for acquiring knowledge of the universe—which is, after all, studying the handiwork of God: "Yet learning itself is not to be blamed, nor is the simple knowledge of anything whatsoever to be despised, for true learning is good in itself and ordained by God."

The Scientific Method in Perspective

More than sixty years ago, I began my quest to become a rocket scientist, pursuing a degree in astrophysics as applied to space flight. My concentration was studying the characteristics of the atmosphere (which exists in attenuated form even in outer space) and its effect on bodies traveling through it at high speed. In my doctoral studies, I was given the assignment of solving a particular set of mathematical equations that I was told others had been unable to solve and that appeared to handle a very complex situation—namely, the heating effect on space vehicles as they reenter the earth's atmosphere. The solution was needed for space travel.

I solved the equations—but the system did not work, in that it produced the wrong answers! I could not find a solution to the problem based on the accepted theories—but at least I had made a contribution to science by proving those theories incorrect. My research director told me that what I had done was enough for my doctorate. But that did not satisfy me, because I had an idea of how to solve the problem with an entirely different approach.

I then found an acceptable solution using an empirical approach based on logic, which fit the scientific observations available. My research director was ecstatic. I was satisfied. I had found truth. Accolades from others and personal satisfaction are always gratifying. But Thomas à Kempis keeps these things in proportion:

> Where are now all those Masters and Doctors whom you knew so well in their lifetime in the full flower of their learning? Other men now sit in their seats, and they are hardly ever called to mind.

Uncertainty Is a Certainty

Here are a few of the realities one lives with as an investigator in the science of jet propulsion and space travel:

Rocket Ships and God

1. Space flight is imponderable, as full of uncertainty now as it was sixty years ago.

2. The unforeseen is always possible, and even likely.

3. Rocket science is an exact science; yet it is built around the phenomenon of error. That is, it is geared heavily to uncertainty and immediate corrective action.

In finance, rocket scientists made their mark on Wall Street and in the world because of their application of mathematical concepts to create fail-safe "hedge" strategies in investments and trades. Space flight deals with the unforeseen and with the improbable. "Uncertainty under time pressure" is another way of saying the same thing.

Consider a car traveling at high speed on an unknown road. There are no headlights, and forward vision is very dim. On the other hand, the rear path is brightly lit and is readily visible to the driver. While bizarre, this scenario is quite similar to how we forecast the future in business, finance, politics, war, and many other things. Why? The lessons of the past are totally available. By manipulating these past results, projections are created for the future. We are plotting the forward path by looking backward.

While we're at it, managing constant uncertainty is also vital in war, diplomacy, politics, medical treatments, research, and almost anything else you can name as a discipline. Anticipating the results of a policy is always a fundamental goal in the decision-making process. It is vital to have some idea of consequences before and after a commitment. But more important is the ability to evaluate unforeseen results, or even errors, and to take corrective action in time. Since we cannot control the total impact of our decisions, the solution is *to control the time interval for corrective action.*

The Scientific Method in Perspective

It sounds ridiculous, doesn't it? Sometimes it works, but often it doesn't, especially on new or unknown "roads." On the other hand, some forms of forecasting work quite reliably, such as weather predictions. Weather is different, however: it moves from west to east as the world spins on its axis. We can see it coming, so the questions are what path it will take and how it will change on the way. We can make some inferences based on the speed with which weather patterns will move eastward, adjusted for how they might be affected by geography (mountains and lakes, for example) and other known influences.

We could say that financial markets work similarly, but in reverse. The trading day begins in the Far East, as Australia, Japan, and China open first in what is midmorning for them; then Europe opens; then lastly, New York and the rest of America. A bad day in the Far East is a significant factor in determining whether the trading day will be bad in New York, at least at the opening bell. But the factors that can quickly take things in a totally different direction are many, and unlike weather, they can change everything in seconds.

A better way must be found to control uncertainty. One natural answer would be to concentrate more closely on the patterns and signals coming from the future. Put brighter headlights on the car. Perhaps! But there is more that is uncertain than can be revealed by brighter lights. A much better answer lies in accepting the uncertainty, accepting the inability to use the past completely to project the future, and in finding ways to *control entry into the future* to avoid catastrophe.

Perhaps the solution lies in providing a control mechanism to keep the car on the road no matter how the road twists and turns, whether you have headlights to reveal it or not, no matter what the speed. Suppose you had a control mechanism continually

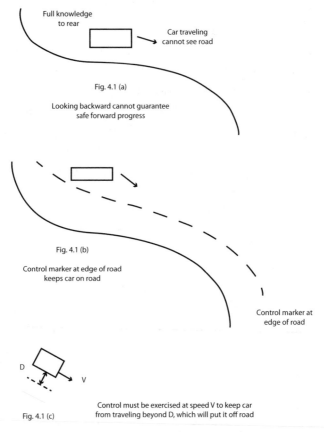

Fig. 4.1 (a)

Looking backward cannot guarantee
safe forward progress

Fig. 4.1 (b)

Control marker at edge of road
keeps car on road

Control marker at
edge of road

Fig. 4.1 (c)

Control must be exercised at speed V to keep car
from traveling beyond D, which will put it off road

Figure 4.1: Car Control System

measuring and keeping the right front wheel a specific distance
from the edge of the road. For that to work, the speed of reaction
must be such that the wheel will not go off the road before the
direction of travel can be adjusted.

That same idea is in our homes everywhere. It is called a thermostat. The temperature is adjusted, and a range of variation is
set. The heating and cooling take place to keep the temperature
at the designated setting within the range prescribed.

The Scientific Method in Perspective

The major difference between a thermostat-type control and the car-type control described is the time element and the risk factor. The thermostat adjusts the temperature, but there is little time pressure in doing so. The response interval is slow. In the car, the response must be quick enough to keep the car on the road. Time is of the essence. But so long as the system responds fast enough, steering the car will be unnecessary. The control system will take care of it!

Such systems, such as the automatic pilot, are used every day in aircraft. They are in everyday use in space for satellites and in manned and unmanned aircraft to control movements at high speed, in order to make minor corrections to the path of travel. This type of system works by what is called negative feedback, in which a signal loops back to counter an aberration of some kind. In a positive-feedback system, the impetus increases a given effect instead of countering it, as, for example, when a man's heart speeds up with exercise. Then he gets tired, which is a negative-feedback system. His sensation of fatigue, touched off by an increase of carbon dioxide in his lungs and lactic acid in his muscles, inspires him to ease up on his exertion.

Control systems, such as a thermostat or an imagined car-control system, continually correct to meet changing conditions. So it must be in forecasting. Foretelling the future in the short as well as the long term has always been the goal. This is an improbable task, but it must be carried out. It is essential to have some idea of consequences before commitment.

Faith and Disillusionment

Something that science and religion share is that they are efforts to foretell what will happen in the future, and why. When I was a boy, I tried to understand why there was light, and why power—and sometimes a tingle!—came from a plug in the wall. And why did water run from a tap when I turned it? I was raised a Catholic and learned my catechism at my mother's knee, with my father, and from the religious sisters who taught me in school. I accepted the Catholic Faith because of my respect and love for those who told me the truth. By the time I reached high school, I even felt I had a vocation to be a Jesuit.

As often happens, all this changed at about the time I entered the university and wondered if God really exists. I had a similar relationship with my fascination for science. I entered an honors course in mathematics, physics, and chemistry. Deeply enmeshed in the rigors of science and its language—mathematics—I came to know how indeterminate and questionable many of the accepted tenets of science are! Anything practiced under the name of "science" is usually assumed to be an objective set of truths. But I soon found out that this is not quite so. Results can be malleable, depending on your frame of reference and the names you use to describe your result. How is it supposed to work?

Defining a Methodology for Science

Let's assume we want to measure the speed of sound. We design and perform a set of experiments and take measurements that include not only our sound-producing and sound-registering devices but the conditions, including the ambient temperature, altitude, and atmospheric pressure. We can even note our height and eye and hair color. We do these things many times to achieve consistency. When the results are in, they appear to be affected only by temperature and pressure (or altitude). The other factors—even our hair color!—have no impact on the speed of sound.

An experiment is designed to be a test of logical connections—especially causal ones—between events or properties of matter. The process is iterative (repeating), looping back as necessary to modify conditions and retest. You can see the process—called an Iterative Feedback Loop—in its simplest form in figure 4.2 (see next page). Let's follow along:

1. The process starts with an *idea* or hypothesis (a proposed explanation of why a thing happens) as shown in box 1. The idea is taken through a *test*—which could be a live experiment or measurement, a mathematical extrapolation based on measurements from a different experiment, or even a logical calculation.

2. Next, we examine our *result*. What happened, and what's the significance of it? Does the result make sense compared with other facts we know? If it suggests a conflict with known facts but represents a credible process, is there possibly a larger principle that would produce both results logically? We adduce reasons for and against the significance of our result by weighing *validity factors* that might sway our opinion one way or the other. We decide if the idea is *valid* or *invalid*.

3. If the idea proves *valid* (box 3), the idea is confirmed; this points to success (box 4).

4. If the idea is *invalid*, our options are to *try again* or *stop*.

5. If we opt to *stop*, we classify the process as a *fail* (box 5).

6. If instead we decide to *try again*, the process feeds back to the beginning through *modify test* or *modify idea* and begins again at box 1.

The Iterative Feedback Loop is the fundamental tool of the scientific method. There can be no conflict between the findings of one discipline and another, so long as the method of

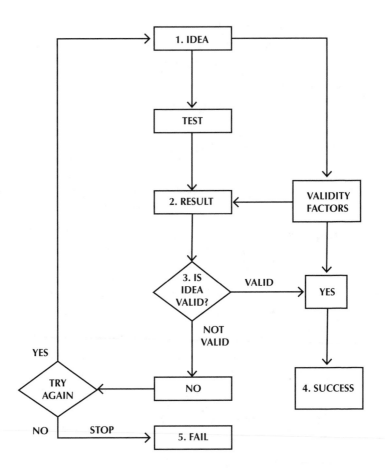

Figure 4.2: General Form of an Iterative Feedback Loop

determination is *verifiable* and *can be duplicated by others*. (As we recall from chapter 2, truth is invariant from one field to another.)

The process can be described in a more fine-grained way. Figure 4.3 (see facing page) is something we might use for our experiment in measuring the speed of sound. As you can see, where physical measurements are concerned, experiments are repeated and observations are made until consistent answers are found (box 7). If consistent answers are found (box 8), then the process is successful (box 12). On the other hand, if no consistent answers are found (box 9), then the whole effort can be recycled or terminated as a *fail* (box 11).

Knowing Everything and Nothing

This seems all rather neat and methodical. It really is not. Much of what we scientists have come up with in the laboratory was

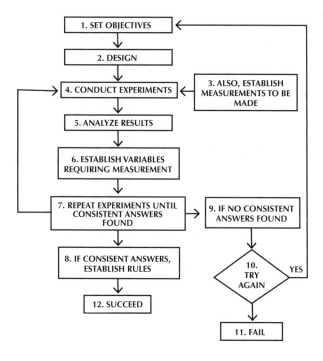

Figure 4.3: Iterative Feedback Loop for an Experiment

based on hunches, testing, explanations, and fitting the test and explanation against fact. But the important thing is not where we got an idea, but whether it works when we test it. We accepted it, testing the approach and premises in the chemistry and physics laboratories as part of our courses of study. We even designed new labs—hypersonic and supersonic wind tunnels, shock tubes, and simulations of travel in outer space.

The results of the scientific method speak for themselves. We have traveled to the moon; we are building a space station; we have nuclear power plants; we can communicate worldwide from anywhere; and we have populated the world with almost as many computers—including cell phones—as we have people. It all seems tangibly real, objective, and comprehensive.

We took our minimum of courses in philosophy, economics, and other disciplines, and came away feeling that those areas of knowledge were subjective, compared with the sciences—just opinions—and that truth in the realm of mere ideas could not be identified.

But it dawned on those of us working in the scientific fields that we could not, and still cannot explain light, magnetism, gravity, electricity, and, most especially, how these major forces are linked—if indeed they are. Seemingly, we can do almost anything, but know almost nothing. We can fix the car, but still have no idea what makes it go.

Liberal Arts

As a nineteen-year-old junior, I asked permission to study philosophy and theology while still maintaining all my science courses. But rather than calm my concerns about the inconsistencies I saw in science and mathematics, these studies initiated more mental gymnastics in me as I now found what seemed to be inconsistencies in religious dogma. I was particularly troubled as I developed rationalist explanations for many traditions of Christianity and Judaism. I was attracted to the theory that visitors from outer space came to Earth and left behind traditions that became convoluted into our sacred Scriptures. (So much for scientifically choosing the simplest hypothesis that explains the facts!)

Despite the continual turmoil in my mind, and perhaps latching on to Pascal's wager, I retained some element of my faith no matter what. I still remember my prayers to God that began with, "If there is a God …" My problem was that like many young men, I was being too cerebral.

It was at this point that I heard the story about St. Augustine of Hippo's (A.D. 354–430) stroll on the beach. This philosopher-theologian could not understand the concept of the Trinity. He pondered long and deeply, trying to resolve his questions with logic. Then one day as he walked along the shore, he saw a little boy carrying a bucket of water from the sea and dumping it into a small hole he had dug in the sand. He saw the boy do this a number of times.

He finally approached the lad and asked him, "Why are you doing that?" The boy gave him a mischievous grin and replied, "I am emptying the ocean into that hole." St. Augustine knew instantly that, just as the boy's hole in the sand could never contain the entire ocean, so Augustine could never grasp the mystery of the Trinity from his struggles in logic alone.

A few decades later, St. Patrick (d. 493) used the shamrock to show Irish pagans how there are three Persons in one God. But he did not explain the Trinity itself. In chapter 1, we saw how we could define the Trinity mathematically with as much "precision" as any science student could wish for, using set theory.

But precision doesn't prove or ultimately explain anything in science, any more than it does in religion.

I accept the Trinity mathematically, philosophically, and theologically. But I still do not understand it! It is a mystery. So are the wave-or-particle nature of light and the existence of magnetism.

The Comfort Syndrome

We are all seekers of comfort—in terms not of ease, but of the absence of fear and a source of strength. It is a zone where we feel secure, serene, confident, strong, and free. We are restless and never really achieve this state, but we search for it as something we seem to believe is there.

We can think of ultimate comfort as a goal for which we strive. The curve approaching this goal is the common S-curve, seen so often in science. Scientifically, we can say that we approach

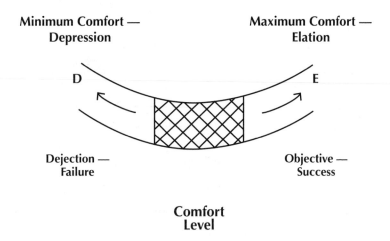

Figure 4.4: The Comfort Syndrome

the ultimate comfort asymptotically, never really reaching it, but coming close or not as we move forward. It is the little steps, the little goals and accomplishments of the day, as St. John Neumann (1811–1860) taught, that make it real.

Perfection

In science, perfection is the goal and is impossible to achieve. The stakes are high. Being 99.9999 percent accurate would appear to be proficient. But in space travel, an error of that magnitude is enough to miss the target and send your craft skipping into the orbit of the wrong planet. All men are imperfect and prone to error and sin. Yet we can proceed in stages toward unity with God—with many ups and downs—as we progress toward our goal.

You could say the cycle of the Iterative Feedback Loop to identify the truth in science is parallel to the process of purifying our soul. There is the *idea*—seeking Christ and increasing detachment from obstacles in our will that get in the way of our unity with Him. But as in the feedback loop in figure 4.3, we spend most of time at box 7: "Repeat experiments until consistent answers found"—that is, until we make consistently perfect responses to God. That pretty much ensures that for most of our lives we'll spend most of our time on this chart over at box 10: "Try again," which we could nickname "Confession." We know where the ultimate goal is, and the stakes are eternal. On this chart, box 12 is called: "Succeed," which seems about right.

In science as in the spiritual life, the summary of many little things leads to the truth. The history of science is replete with discoveries made through accidents and through details that could have been overlooked, but weren't. A key left on a photographic key holder led to the discovery of X-rays. Apparent errors in the measurement in the speed of light and the parahelion of the planet Mercury led to the Theory of Relativity. And as we recounted, perturbations of the orbit of the planet Uranus led to the prediction and successful searches for Neptune and Pluto.

There is only one difference, really, between the scientific method and the methods of theology: the source of the original premise. (A feedback loop diagram describing the scientific method is shown in figure 4.5.) In other respects, philosophy, theology, physics, and all science are simply different branches of knowledge.

The approach toward perfection or ultimate truth shown in figure 4.6 is certainly asymptotic. It can represent the perfecting of human beings as well as the growth of the body of truth in all of science.

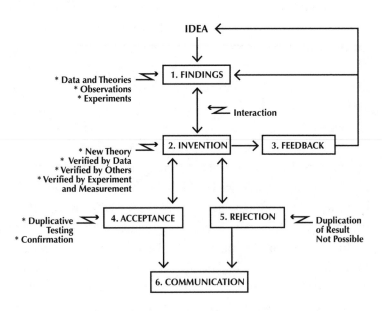

Figure 4.5: Simplified Diagram of Scientific Method

5

The Truth Is One:
On Proving God's Existence

How do we know the truth when we see it?

Bernard Lonergan, S.J., was a Canadian priest trained in science, philosophy, and theology. His goal was to extend the work of St. Thomas Aquinas to unify human knowledge. Whereas St. Thomas applied the thinking of Aristotle as a tool to deepen our understanding of Christ and creation, Lonergan aimed to put modern scientific and historical insights to the service of Christian thought. He was responding to the explosion of scientific knowledge unleashed in the twentieth century — which had produced marvels, epic wars and bloodshed, and a kaleidoscope of new insights that seemed to some to throw into question old ways of living, common sense, and the very fear of God. Echoing Einstein's goal of a Unified Field Theory to unify and organize the findings of physics, Lonergan wanted to create a Generalized Empirical Method (GEM) to discover and describe the truth and human perception of it.

One task Lonergan undertook was to separate *objective* human understanding from *subjective* human understanding. Lonergan is sometimes associated with a movement toward "Transcendental Thomism" first initiated by Belgian Jesuit Joseph Marechal. You could describe it as being skeptical about what we really know, or even what we *can* know, unless we systematically make ourselves aware of what *other* things we know and feel that affect our perception—which can be obstacles to our objectivity. To know what we're talking about—and to understand what God really has created—we have to know *how we know* what we know.

The GEM divides human knowing into three levels: *experience*, *understanding*, and *judgment*. It goes beyond German philosopher Immanuel Kant (1724–1804), who believed that objective truth was knowable, in showing *how* objectivity in judgment can be cultivated and identified. What we see, think, or are conscious of can be affected by our personality, our family and friends, and historical developments. In order to know what is objectively true, it is crucial to understand the mental and emotional landscape through which we perceive it.

Lonergan has a method for rooting out our perception biases. It consists of eight steps or functions that should be used in forming and improving an argument or theological claim. His first four steps concern the past—research, history, interpretation, and dialectic. The second four concern the future: foundations, doctrines, systematics, and communication.

In figure 5.1, each of these steps (boxes 1–8) simply feeds directly into the next—except for the first four boxes. Those are about defining the problem, so it's not surprising that insights from some of them may influence the others—hence the arrows back and forth between them.

1. *Research*. This encompasses whatever information is available, from any source. St. Thomas drew on Aristotle, the Church Fathers and Doctors, and his own colleagues. As we pointed out in an earlier chapter,

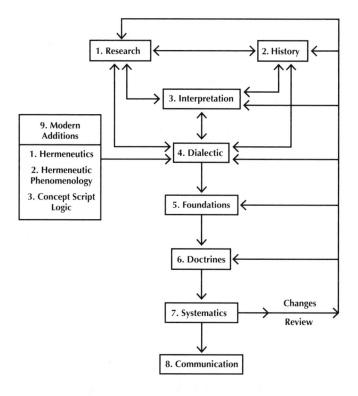

Figure 5.1: Functions in the Basic Lonergan Method
— with Modern Additions

St. Thomas's access to Aristotle was crucially helped by Averroës' earlier commentaries and translations of Aristotle. Writing in 1972, Lonergan dreamed of "a complete information-retrieval system"[12] that would make research of all kinds easier and more complete. Has his dream been realized through the search engines of the Internet?

[12]Lonergan, *Method in Theology*, 127.

2. *Interpretation.* Philosophers often agree on the translation of a document but disagree on its meaning. In this step, we vet different possible interpretations and the consequences of the differences.

3. *History.* The history of words and phraseology takes on great significance. The meaning of words often shifts through the ages—for example, the use of *honest* in Shakespearean plays. In the Elizabethan Era, the connotation was of a particular *kind* of honesty—chastity. Another example is the use of the word *gay* as a synonym for *homosexual*, whereas only a few years ago, it simply meant lighthearted.

4. *Dialectic.* In dialectic, we illuminate an idea by comparing it with its polar opposite. In Lonergan's words, "dialectic has to do with the concrete, the dynamic, and the contradictory."[13] He stresses differences, including criticism, in order to purge reasoning that is unsound.

5. *Foundations.* The process of defining the problem and examining evidence leads to foundations, where we put our proposed solution. From our perspective of today, the findings of steps 1 through 4 lead to the foundation for moving forward to a new, different, or broader conclusion; and from a modern systems-engineering perspective, this is the final definition of the problem.

6. *Doctrines.* This is the step of implementation of the solution—doctrine being the implementation of a

[13]Lonergan, *Method in Theology*, 129.

theological idea. These are the conclusions of a theological investigation and "express judgments of fact and judgments of value."[14]

7. *Systematics.* Step 7 is review and modification—grooming the system. This is the place for feedback and modifying premises and conclusions in the light of further information. Feedback can be used to alter even the initial question.

8. *Communication.* Here is theology's connection to the external world and the cycle's completion: the dissemination, proclamation, or explanation of the idea. Lonergan identifies three recipients or partners of this communication: (1) interdisciplinary realms of knowledge, including other religions; (2) science; (3) philosophy and history. In today's world, communication must certainly include the use of electronic media as well as print and visual. Not only is modern communication universal and immediate, but it also provides the capacity for dialogue and theological collaboration "in real time."

9. *Modern additions.* This extra step offers additional modern "lenses" through which we can look at our argument, such as hermeneutics, hermeneutic phenomenology, and concept script logic. On the chart, it's not at the end but next to box 4!

Modern computer-centered search and communication capability has extended the usefulness of Lonergan's method

---

[14]Ibid., 37.

substantially. We can consider linking it with the scientific method to provide a uniform approach for any problem in any discipline. Just as the ancients used their observations of the natural world around them in their philosophy, we can pull facts and insights from any discipline.

A Unified Method of Truth Collection

This concept can lead to a unified approach to all branches of knowledge in finding the truth. Scientific evidence and facts can be used in theological investigation—and vice versa! What is the implication of that? Essentially, religion is an accumulation of the rituals and understandings associated with our desire to honor and unite ourselves to an all-knowing and all-loving God. To paraphrase Pope Benedict XVI, faith is our attempt to look beyond the present and beyond the barriers of life itself, into the future.

But all truth is one. With the unifying of knowledge, the mathematically inspired insights offered by the scientific method might allow us to understand more about God and His creation than we have ever imagined.

How shall we begin our open-ended search for truth, whether our source is observation, experimentation, intuition, revelation, or divine intervention? Let's start with something easy—say, a proof for the existence of God.

To guide our examination, I propose a system even broader than Lonergan's GEM that I have devised, which I call Unifying Theology and Science (UTS) In figure 5.2, I sketch a quick tour of UTS in the form of yet another cycle chart—this one designed pretty much to encompass them all—whose task is to incorporate and process knowledge from *all* sources.

We start at 1: *idea.* The idea, assertion, or question will be developed and tested, not merely to reach a conclusion, but if

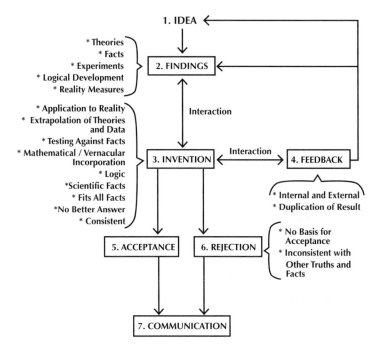

Figure 5.2: Which Discipline Is Not Germane? (They All Are.)

it passes muster, to transmit it somehow to the world. The goal at the end is labeled *communication*.

As with our other cycle charts, an idea may be rejected along the way to be modified or abandoned entirely. Or an idea could, in a sense, beat the system: As the idea goes through examinations and experiments in *findings* (box 2), *invention* (box 3), and *feedback* (box 4), the ultimate result might turn out to be that the idea inspires us to modify our premises, and we start the cycle again. The conclusion at *communication* can lead to proclamation of a dogma, rule, brilliant insight, invention, or failure.

Rocket Ships and God

You may remember that in chapter 2, we did a simplified proof for the existence of God. We can now examine that solution somewhat differently.

The Question of God

Whether we are religious, atheist, or something in between, what do we rationally mean by God? The expression would have to mean a power beyond our comprehension and logic, a power not subject to the laws of nature as we know them or can now imagine them.

It is my opinion that explaining the origin of the universe as the result of chance and the development of life as a product of evolution are valid theories. It is also my opinion that they could have been *used* by a supernatural force outside nature (God). So, as explanations, neither chance nor evolution in itself logically excludes God.

But let's take things back a step. The chance answer has a problem right out of the gate. Scientifically, we know that entropy—the tendency of matter to go from a state of high potential energy (order) to low (chaos)—never decreases. Hence, energy is always static or increasing as matter is converted into energy. But that makes our question all the more confounding. Matter exists. If random chance (entropy) tends to consume matter by converting it to energy, how could chance result in matter? Where did matter come from?

Chance might dictate *which* matter might be converted into energy, but chance could never *establish* matter initially. Nor could chance *create* the continuing law in natural science—or physics—on how matter and energy are intertwined by Einstein's famous discovery: $e = mc^2$. (In case you've forgotten: e is energy, m is mass, and c is the speed of light.)

The Truth Is One

Einstein's equation puts our finger on a vital concept concerning the formation of the universe: it proves that the initial, enormous mass *could* have been created from an equally enormous — quasi-infinite — amount of energy. That would be the scenario for the Big Bang — where an enormous mass concentrated at a point began to expand to create the universe and has expanded ever since. The bang doesn't refer to an explosion per se (the term *Big Bang* is a bit of a misnomer), but there was a single, initial point from which the universe expanded — the center of the "Big Bang."

On the other hand, some consider the cosmos as always having been there, with *no beginning*. While this runs contrary to our cerebral sense of what is possible, we must consider it as an alternative. Carl Sagan was world famous for writing popular science books and for cowriting and presenting the 1980 PBS television series *Cosmos: A Personal Voyage*, which was seen by more than six hundred million people in over sixty countries.

Sagan, in his book *Cosmos*[15] and in his teaching career, posited the theory that there was always a cosmos. He accepted the Big Bang, not as a starting event of great magnitude and importance but as an event within the infinite and cylindrical life cycle of the cosmos.[16]

Nobel laureate Stephen Hawking leans toward the same approach but places more stress on what happened *after* the Big Bang. Neither one would agree that a Creator existed, much less that He exists today. They and others have taken

[15]Carl Sagan, *Cosmos* (New York: Random House, 1980).
[16]Mathematical formulae can be generated that show an infinite, cylindrical space; others suggest that a vast number of parallel universes exist. But these are unproven manipulations of invented mathematical theories.

the position that there are laws of science that we do not as yet understand that can explain phenomena—but without resort to belief in a supernatural force or God who might have written those laws.

Calling us to embrace their faith in science without a God, Sagan and Hawking ask us to believe that the cosmos suddenly happened or that it was somehow *always there*. (Something present for all eternity doesn't seem improbable to them, as long as it wasn't God.)

It seems strange, almost bizarre, that brilliant, thoughtful men would put their faith in unproven and unlikely answers, when a logical answer is right there before them. But since even naysayers and agnostics accept the concept of the Big Bang, let us eagerly take it as a point of agreement.

The Big Bang presupposes a very large mass, continually expanding from a single point as if it had exploded instantaneously, scattering matter throughout the universe, creating the planets and the stars as we know them—and further, that the process of expansion is still going on. According to calculations, the transition from nothing to an expanding universe occurred in 10^{-43} seconds.

If we assume this is what happened, then where did the mass come from? We could presuppose that the mass was created from an enormous—almost infinite—energy field, but where did the energy originate? Neither Sagan, nor Hawking, nor anyone else who believes in an "always there" universe has an answer.

In our natural law, something cannot come from nothing. If it does, then we are at the point where we must admit that we are dealing with something outside all natural law, science, and reason as we know them. We can refer to "it" as the "supernatural" or even "supranatural"—outside nature—but there is nothing in logic or reason to oppose us in calling that supernatural force God.

The more we study the cosmos, especially through the use of the Hubble Telescope in space, the more this becomes evident. The more we learn of the almost infinite space of the universe, the more we question how it all came to be. We can take pictures of stars forty billion light years away. We can estimate the age of the universe as about fourteen billion years. We can quantify the number of stars and galaxies in the billions. Our observations have even determined that the expansion of space from the point of the Big Bang is so great that in future millennia, the ability to discern the effects of the Big Bang will be difficult. Hence, the age of the cosmos and its size lend credibility to the concept of *infinity*—which in our theological analyses we call *eternity*.

There is much accepted truth in scientific observation. Can that truth help us verify or establish philosophical and theological truth? And could we then use that truth to answer some of the great questions that have puzzled mankind for eons?

In its simplest terms, if A = C and B = C, then A = B. Based on that, we can move on to other factors. Mathematically speaking, in Euclidean geometry, when a theorem or proposition is proved, it is proven. For example, most of us were taught the Pythagorean theorem: in a right triangle, the square of the hypotenuse is always equal to the sums of the squares of the other two sides. Forever! It is invariant: the size of the triangle, its location, the units we use to measure it, and the language in which we discuss it are all immaterial. So long as the triangle has a right angle, this proposition is always true. Likewise, perceptions, feelings, and beliefs have no basis in whether this theorem is true. Once you've seen it proved, the situation is fairly obvious, almost cut and dried.

Rocket Ships and God

The UTS Process

The process begins not with a search for God but with a definition of a scientific theory associated with the creation of the universe, such as the Big Bang Theory. This theory is a favorite of atheists since it does not (they suppose) logically necessitate a grand design for the universe. As an act of faith in the validity of this explanation, we are to believe that all the forces that regulate the entire universe sprang into being automatically. We know how finely tuned the universe is, with the balanced forces of gravity, thermonuclear processes in the stars, finely tuned life cycles (at least on our planet), and myriad examples of an elegant discoverable structure throughout. All studies of the cosmos throughout history have revealed this order and elegance, even the powerful, relentlessly detailed studies of the modern age—which have ranged from the subatomic to the intergalactic.

Be that as it may, let us at least assume the theory to be valid—that everything started from a single point in space some 13.7 billion years ago; and in 10^{-43} seconds a gigantic mass, containing all the matter in the universe, started expanding.

Applying UTS to this theory, the following can be stated:

Findings
Research

1. The universe is expanding. This is determined by measuring shifts in the light from distant galaxies.

2. The more distant the galaxies, the faster they appear to be moving outward—i.e., expanding.

3. Galaxies can be traced backward to a common point from which they seem to have come. That is the essence of the Big Bang.

4. By tracing the speed of expansion of galaxies and estimating the distance to the origin point, the age of the universe can be calculated.

5. In the Theory of Relativity proposed by Einstein in 1905, the equation $e = mc^2$ linked energy, mass and the speed of light.

6. The speed of light has been assumed to be a constant — about 186,262 miles per second. Recent experiments at the international astrophysics laboratory CERN in Geneva, Switzerland, provide some indication that the speed of light might not be constant and furthermore that the speed of light is *not* a constraining limit to the speed of particles. If this is true, then conceivably the age of the universe might be somewhat different from what is currently proposed.

7. The functioning of the atomic bomb and nuclear energy verify the equation proposed by Einstein, where enormous energy came from a relatively small weight of fissionable uranium 235 or plutonium.

Interpretation

1. If $e = mc^2$, then $m = e/c^2$

Hence, mass can be created from an energy source.

2. The amount of energy needed to create the mass of the entire universe is enormous, quasi-infinite.

3. A quasi-infinite energy source cannot come from nothing. None of the laws of physics as we know them can account for this energy field.

4. There is a mathematical and scientific basis for considering an expanding universe and a common starting point.

5. Scripture is historical. For some it is divinely inspired. For everyone, however, it stands as universal attempts over cycles of time to answer the basic question of where it all came from. Is the Creator defined completely in Scripture? Hardly! Scripture was written by different writers over centuries. Some sections, such as Genesis, are heavily allegorical. Others, such as the letters of Paul, are quite logical; while the Gospels attributed to Matthew, Mark, Luke, and John are historic documents on the life and teachings of Jesus Christ. They were not disputed by those who lived at that time. Hence we take as literal only that which we know is valid and treat as allegorical such things as the "days" in Genesis, which could represent eons of time.

History

1. Alternative theories for the origination of the universe are:

    a. The universe is the product of supranatural forces; i.e., a Creator with a grand design.

    b. The universe suddenly emerged from nothing. A recent book, *A Universe from Nothing*, by Lawrence Krauss, professor and director of the Origins Project at Arizona State University in Tempe, Arizona, goes to great lengths to speak of "nothing" as a form of nascent matter. Common sense would indicate that his "nothing" really is something, as he states in his book. He does admit that the universe is "full of stuff." He questions how it got there. Without any proof, he asserts that it all resulted from a natural process that is unknown. He refers to Darwin's theory that diversity of life can arise from these same unknown natural causes. His conclusions are absurd scientifically, demanding blind faith in a scientific truth that has no basis in the Scientific Method.

Darwin's Theory of Evolution itself is questionable scientifically. There is no known mechanism by which the E coli bacterium's flagellum could have evolved. There are studies that rather definitively suggest that this particular microbe could not evolve but either was or was not.

The same is true of the universe. It was or was not. It did not evolve. Was it the product of design by a greater power than any we can comprehend, or of laws of science that are outside anything we know or can reasonably conceive? Either way, it is supranatural.

    c.   The universe all came out of nothing by chance. There is no scientific form or basis for this assertion. Hence, even in this scenario, a supranatural force is indicated.

2. There is no scientific basis for assuming the universe came from nothing by chance.

3. Reason throughout history leads to the belief in love of the Creator for us creatures. This becomes apparent as we delve deeper and deeper into the mystique of the beauty of nature — including the universal recognition

of beauty itself as a trait—and the phenomenon of mankind.

4. It is logical to assume a Creator. It is illogical to posit a phenomenon with no cause.

5. It may be claimed that some future discovery will make it possible for the laws of science and logic to accept something coming from nothing, by chance. This seems unlikely.

6. It comes down to a question of faith in a Creator who has left a complex universe as His calling card or faith in an unknown science that is yet to be detected. The logical possibility that the unknown, undetected science that, according to atheists, created the universe is in fact the toolbox of the same Creator described by religious revelation seems almost unavoidable.

Dialectic

1. The mass necessary for the entire universe would require a quasi-infinite energy source if indeed the mass came from energy.

2. Even if everything "started" with a single large mass that expanded, and is still expanding, there is the question of what came before then; and where the single large mass originated.

3. There is currently no scientific theory in any discipline that can account for a quasi-infinite energy source suddenly existing.

4. Does a Creator exist? It is logical to assume so, in that we are surrounded by a creation—persistently

The Truth Is One

existing phenomena. Reason tells me that there is a Creator. Further reasoning, especially through the lens of String Theory, puts forth the premise that time could have existed before the Big Bang. That has been a theological argument for some time — that the Creator always "was" (see John 1). Scientifically, we are leaning more and more toward the idea of curved time as well as curved space. In this the premises of both theology and science are coming to the same conclusion.

5. Reason allows us to identify certain characteristics of the Creator. By the same logic as some assert that there is no Creator, characterizations of a Creator can be accepted on reason or faith either because they are proven, or because there is no better answer, or because we believe them to be true.

6. The existence of a Creator, a supranatural Being, or God is buttressed by the findings in many disciplines of truth.

7. Can we know much about the Creator? Only what is revealed to us, and what we can glean from observing the Creator's works. As with the phenomenon of light, we know the effects, but we do not know precisely how or why. We accept light. Can we accept a Creator?

8. Our minds indicate a Creator exists. Logic says a Creator exists. Faith leads us to accept, even if we cannot understand. Love was certainly a reason for us to exist — both the love of our parents and by inference the love of the Creator of us all.

9. As children we sang: "Jesus loves me—this we know; 'cause the Bible tells me so." Logically we know this is true.

10. Mankind has sought answers to these questions from the dawn of history.

11. There has always been some form of belief in supernatural forces or gods.

12. The Egyptians, Greeks, and Romans developed an extensive mythology of divinity—forces beyond nature and beyond their reason.

Invention

Foundation: Nothing disproves the existence of God.

1. The universe may have started with the Big Bang.

2. We can discern the attributes of God from what God has created.

Doctrine: God exists.

1. Whether from an energy-mass conversion or by chance, the creation of the universe came about from forces outside the realm of all nature, knowledge, or reason as we know or can conceive them.

2. That supranatural or supernatural force we will call God.

Systematics: There is no better answer.

1. An enormous amount of matter was needed for the universe to exist.

2. This matter could have come from energy. If so, this requires a quasi-infinite energy source.

3. The speed of light may or may not be a constant.

Communication: God exists.

At this time, there is no better answer to the question of the creation of the universe than to conclude the existence of God. No other answer has been described. It is doubtful that any other credible answer now exists and no indication of how another could be proven.

The Question of God: Summary

From the dawn of history, mankind wondered how the universe came to be. Solutions were sought by logical analyses of ideas, on one hand, and measurement and observation on the other. The realms of philosophy and science progressed separately. In the twentieth century, electronic information systems and immediate communication capability brought together the people and the findings in many disciplines for immediate communication on any specific problem or issue. Visualization techniques, when added to computer and communication capability, provided the third part of a Cyber Triad capable of being applied to any premise. The question of God can be considered using any and all scientific accepted findings. Applying the fundamental linkage relationship between energy, mass, and the speed of light to the question of God results in a positive conclusion that the universe was created by a God of infinite power, a God who existed before the universe.

UTS: An Appraisal

Uniting the scientific method with theology must, of course, include the replication, especially by others, of all observations and experimental results; and of logical analyses and historical research like the above analysis of creation and of the existence of God.

It is scientifically licit and logical to extrapolate from scientific findings to reveal currently unknown common ground that joins two theories or sets of equations—each of which is accepted in its separate area. (This formed part of the basis of my doctoral dissertation.) It is my hope that this extrapolation approach can be used to create a uniform set of relationships for all realms in science. It is also my opinion that Einstein's dream of a unified theory can be achieved by linking the various realms of science—including theology—into a cohesive whole through a method such as UTS.

The universe is not divided into disciplines of activity such as theology, gravity, electromagnetism, and light. The universe, and everything within it, operates with all these forces and elements as a single, cohesive entity. We divide the scientific universe into disciplines only because the finite nature and narrow scope of any single human mind make it necessary to do so.

We have done well in proceeding as far as we have with our diverse methods of description, whether in words, symbols, or logic; but it is only in the infinite nature of God's mind that the complex nature of the entire universe becomes evident. Man, though made in His image and likeness, for now can only fathom a minute part of why, how, and what we are.

Appendix

A Truth Revealed through Space Travel

I had always dreamed of flying, so at twenty-two, working on space travel at the Institute of Aerospace Studies at the University of Toronto was my fantasy made real. In 1952, we knew, or thought we knew, a great deal about outer space, but we knew very little about space *flight*, especially about the border zone that all space vehicles would have to traverse on their journey out and on their return home: Earth's upper atmosphere. The air up there is very thin — but even so, would the high speed of the vehicle on reentry cause friction with air molecules and heat so intense that it would destroy the craft and its occupants?

My objective in my dissertation was to come up with a way to predict the conditions space vehicles would encounter in the upper atmosphere, especially on reentry from space, which would be crucial in the design of heat shields for space vehicles.

Because of the scant and in some cases faulty data then available, in the end I had to pursue a strategy of linking two unrelated truths to find a third. Truth is discovered through a balance between mind, method, and faith — and faith was critical in this case. I had to trust in the truthfulness of the scientific method and also in the orderly design of the physical universe that it was designed to reveal. I needed faith that a solution to my problem existed that would meet all the known observations, allowing me to make a projection that could be tested.

Since the nineteenth century, we had relied on the calculations of motion called the Navier-Stokes equations. These describe the collisions between the molecules of atmospheric gases with a body passing through them. But the Navier-Stokes equations apply only to the relatively dense atmosphere of sea level.

Meanwhile, the Maxwell equations, first discovered in the eighteenth century and perfected in the nineteenth, deal mainly with electromagnetic phenomena—but they also were found to apply to molecular motion in a rarefied atmosphere—that is, where there are far fewer air molecules per cubic volume of space than there are at sea level. In a thin-air environment, air molecules are more likely to collide with a body traveling through them at high speed than with other air molecules!

Further, a key factor called the Knudsen number is the distance a molecule will travel before it collides with another molecule in a given volume of space, divided by the dimensions of a body traveling through that space.

The subject assigned to me for my doctoral dissertation was a hot (sorry!) topic. It was vital in the search for heat shields, which later proved critical to the success of the *Mercury*, *Gemini* and *Apollo* programs. But it required bringing together all those equations and matching them to the real world.

The director of our institute, Dr. Gordon Neal Patterson (known to us as GNP or the Doc) had been working on the issue of reentry of space vehicles into the atmosphere. He had become very concerned, due to the high temperatures involved, about the safe recovery of astronauts. Remember, this was 1952;

there were no astronauts, and no one would even attempt space flight for nearly a decade. But GNP was right to be concerned. When a reentering vehicle runs into atmospheric gas molecules at high speed, it creates a shock wave, compressing the gases. This causes the gas molecules to collide with each other in a dense continuum and to heat up so intensely — to 3,000 degrees Fahrenheit or more — that they become no longer molecules but a plasma. If we sent a vehicle into space to explore the planets and stars, how would we prevent it from turning into a flaming meteor on the return trip?

The job of a heat shield, part of a Thermal Protective System (TPS), is to keep that hot gas from burning up the vehicle. One of the main TPS strategies is *ablative*, whereby the vehicle reenters the atmosphere leading with a blunt (rather than streamlined) surface. This pushes such a wide front of air before it that the hot gases pass by the craft before they can conduct heat to it. That ablative system was used in the later *Mercury* capsules and in the *Gemini* and *Apollo* vehicles. An *adiabatic* is to reflect the heat away from the vehicle — which was used in the United States' early *Mercury* capsules and much later in the space shuttle.[17]

The more Dr. Patterson described the challenge, the more intrigued I became. The approach that the National Advisory

---

[17]One of the disadvantages of the tiles used to make of the reflective carbon shield in the space shuttle is that they are fragile. Unfortunately, we all remember that in 2003, during the launch of the space shuttle *Columbia*, some tiles were knocked off the craft by booster material. As the shuttle began to reenter Earth's atmosphere, heat was able to penetrate the vehicle, and *Columbia* incinerated over several Southern states, killing all seven astronauts aboard.

Rocket Ships and God

Committee for Aeronautics (NACA), the forerunner of NASA, was advocating, did not work. "NACA has given up on this approach," Dr. Patterson said. "Why don't you take a crack at it?" My project had to do with the "slip regime." This is the broad region between sea level and the reaches of outer space. Not that long ago, we believed that outer space was a complete vacuum, but such is not the case. The density of air particles there is a trillionth what it is at sea level, but it is not a vacuum; it is what is called a rarefied atmosphere.

In 1952, there was much interest in space vehicles, manned and unmanned, yet there existed little data on the makeup of the atmosphere and even less knowledge about the composition of outer space. We also knew nothing about the equations of motion above sea level. These equations would have to be formulated before even contemplating space flight.

The problem that NACA had given up on was creating a unified way to determine the heating effect on a spacecraft moving from sea level to outer space and back—especially back. The heating effect would be a function of the speed of the craft and the density of the air at the various altitudes through which the vehicle moved.

The accepted approach from NACA, called the Rayleigh Method, assumed two sets of complex equations: one to cover flight in outer space and another for flight at sea level. My point of study was the slip regime between them. My innate belief was that a single set of equations should cover the entire range from sea level to outer space and back. At that time, no one had developed such a solution—and as far as I know, that is still the case.

Conventional wisdom was to take the equations for sea level and include variations to cover the transition through the slip area into outer space. That involved complex differential equations, plus a further set of differential equations as boundary conditions. This was complex mathematics indeed!

After two years of great labor, I seemingly solved the problem by the Rayleigh Method, using the complex set of existing formulas. But try as I might, I could not solve the problem with a "closed" solution—that is, a set of formulas or equations that could generate the values I needed to calculate the heating effect of reentry. I ended up instead with a set of very complex expressions that I had to solve numerically.

I ended up inventing an assortment of numerical techniques to solve it. I used the new FERUT computer at the University of Toronto, and it worked! But when I rechecked my work using the university's powerful computer system, painstakingly plotting the curves, I found ... a discontinuity. There was a flaw in my design. It had produced two sets of curves that did not meet! The solution did not work after all.

After more detailed analysis, it became evident why. The equations worked at sea level, and the boundary conditions worked in outer space. But there was no connection between the two sets of equations. The curves in figure 1 show that the two theories at each end of the slip regime between sea level and outer space are individually correct; but they cannot predict the correct outcome for that part of the flight in the middle! The Rayleigh Method could not predict the area of great concern for space flight—beyond sea level and before outer space. This was the area of greatest heating of a rapidly moving space vehicle. No amount of mathematical trickery with boundary conditions could make it work.

I was disconsolate. But GNP told me, "Negative results are almost as good as positive ones. You proved NACA was right in abandoning that method, even if they didn't know why."

GNP said what I had done was enough for a Ph.D., but I was not satisfied. I told him, with an engineer's stubborn patience, "I didn't solve the problem."

I went back to my calculations and my computer and began puzzling it out. I had two sets of equations that worked at the extremes of the slip regime: at sea level and in the near vacuum of space. I started to fill in the gaps between. I solved for varying conditions, one after the other, and found the solutions created a curve on which all the experimental points essentially fit. This time, I really *had* solved the problem—the old-fashioned way, slogging through it bit by bit.

We were all elated. GNP called his buddies at NACA and convinced them to give my solution a try in designing heat shields for space flights. I assume he spoke to his close friend Hugh Dryden, after whom NASA's Dryden Flight Research Center is named.

I had succeeded in my task by persisting through many obstacles. By being willing to depart from conventional wisdom, I had found a solution. At least my predictions fell in line with the few observations available then.

In 2000, I attended a doctoral presentation on slip flow at Drexel University in Philadelphia. I listened carefully to see what had happened in fifty years. I was both elated and chagrined. No progress had been made on analyzing the heating effect on reentry from space since my work in the 1950s. Once a solution was found for shielding astronauts from heat—namely, a heat shield—apparently no one saw the need to probe further and create an equation that could rigorously predict what was happening throughout reentry and why.

Another possible reason why the question hasn't been formally pursued is that, with so many space probes and flights since the 1960s, there is now a huge database of observations that can generate real curves based on in-flight measurements. While I was, and am, interested in a hard, theoretical formula that would elegantly and seamlessly predict the correct heat effect once the variables were plugged in, I agree it is best to move on, provided an acceptable solution is at hand.

My dissertation work is important not only for its contribution to the design of heat shields for the space program but also as a starting point for concepts of creating unified theories to be applied to science and to the general pursuit of the truth.

I believe that truth can be represented by piecing together the elements that we know to be true into a mosaic similar to what I am proposing in science. I have proposed this as an empirical approach for developing equations to link the mathematical descriptions (equations) not merely of different altitudes above the earth but of diverse scientific disciplines—in other words, linking diverse truths to find a new truth. That was the thesis not only for my doctorate but for all searches for truth, in which intuitively we sense that there is linkage between knowledge or truths but cannot establish that linkage except by filling the gaps through an empirical approach, and this might make a more comprehensive theory emerge.

This is the Unifying Theology and Science (UTS) Method at work and in discovery. It is the extension of Lonergan's Generalized Empirical Method to all disciplines of knowledge, not just theology. I believe it can be the path toward future breakthroughs in linking the truths of science, philosophy, theology, and all the other branches of science. I believe it will impact religion and philosophy as well as scientific research and discovery.

After all, truth is truth, or it would not be true.

About the Author

Rocco Leonard Martino received his Ph.D. from the Institute of Aerospace Studies of the University of Toronto in 1954 for his work on hazards from atmospheric heating in returning space vehicles, which contributed to the development of heat shields for spacecraft.

At the same time, he took courses in philosophy, theology, and history at St. Michael's College, also part of the University of Toronto. His professors there included Marshall McLuhan and Jacques Maritain.

An inventor of the smartphone, Dr. Martino worked in the finance industry, where the company he founded, XRT, Inc., pioneered the creation of systems for electronic funds transfer and risk management for global companies.

He has served on numerous corporate and foundation boards and was awarded Papal Knighthood in the Order of St. Gregory the Great by Pope John Paul II.

He has written numerous books on technology, religion, and politics.

An Invitation

Reader, the book that you hold in your hands was published by Sophia Institute Press. Sophia Institute seeks to nurture the spiritual, moral, and cultural life of souls and to spread the Gospel of Christ in conformity with the authentic teachings of the Roman Catholic Church.

Our press fulfills this mission by offering translations, reprints, and new publications that afford readers a rich source of the enduring wisdom of mankind.

We also operate two popular online Catholic resources: CrisisMagazine.com and CatholicExchange.com.

Crisis Magazine provides insightful cultural analysis that arms readers with the arguments necessary for navigating the ideological and theological minefields of the day. *Catholic Exchange* provides world news from a Catholic perspective as well as daily devotionals and articles that will help you to grow in holiness and live a life consistent with the teachings of the Church.

Sophia Institute Press also serves as the publisher for the Thomas More College of Liberal Arts and Holy Spirit College. Both colleges provide university-level education under the guiding light of Catholic teaching. If you know a young person seeking a college that takes seriously the adventure of learning and the quest for truth, please bring these institutions to his attention.

www.SophiaInstitute.com
www.CatholicExchange.com
www.CrisisMagazine.com

Sophia Institute Press® is a registered trademark of Sophia Institute. Sophia Institute is a tax-exempt institution as defined by the Internal Revenue Code, Section 501(c)(3). Tax I.D. 22-2548708.